Exceeding
Expectations

Exceeding Expectations

THE HISTORY AND HOPES OF
VIEWPOINT HOUSING ASSOCIATION

Laurence Wareing

Published by
Viewpoint Housing Association Ltd
4 South Oswald Road
Edinburgh
Scotland
EH9 2HG

Phone: 0131 668 4247
Fax: 0131 662 0700
Email: admin@viewpoint.org.uk

First published in 2008

A catalogue record of this book is
available from the British Library.

ISBN: 978-0-9559427-0-9

A large format edition is also available:
ISBN: 978-0-9559427-1-6

Designed by Mark Blackadder

Printed and bound by
MPG Books Ltd
Bodmin
Cornwall
United Kingdom

Contents

Introduction

I sensed that Viewpoint is an organisation keen to go places the moment I arrived for an interview to become the new Chief Executive. A panel of four very committed and enthusiastic members of the Management Committee left me in no doubt that this was a place where I wanted to work. Their knowledge of the housing movement and the care industry was certainly impressive; however, it was their questions about how I would drive Viewpoint into the future that really hooked me. This feeling remained as I came here to take up the Chief Executive post. The quintessential Viewpoint hospitality alluded to in the opening chapter of this 60th Anniversary history was abundantly evident to me, but alongside this was the modern day professionalism of staff and an overwhelming desire to move forward and take Viewpoint into the next phase of its evolution. What an opportunity.

Looking ahead to a landmark anniversary of 60 years' existence caused us to deliberate on how to celebrate this. In the spirit of involvement that has been the trademark of Viewpoint since its inception, a group of willing volunteers, including staff and tenants, got together and plotted in advance a whole range of activities which would involve everyone getting a chance to join in at some point in the year.

One of our hopes was to produce a book that would tell the story of how Scotland's oldest Housing Association came about. An external author was commissioned to look freshly at the organisation on behalf of Viewpoint and it is such a pleasure to see the project come to fruition. We are also very fortunate to receive sponsorship from the Royal Bank of Scotland, which made the whole project possible.

One of the advantages of writing an introduction to the book with the text in front of you is that one has the benefit of perusing the researcher's work and the ability to look back and reflect upon some of the issues it covers. Among other realisations, it makes me aware of how far Viewpoint has travelled in the past two and a half years since I arrived at the organisation. A privilege indeed.

'Change' has been the most constant word in recent times. Both the housing and care industries have been influenced and affected by a number of factors. These include European legislation, the formation of a Scottish Parliament (now Government), and the establishment of regulators such as the Office of Scottish Charities Regulator, Communities Scotland (now the Scottish Housing Regulator), and the Scottish Commission for the Regulation of Care and the Scottish Social Services Council – to name but a few.

All of these developments have served to drive change in recent years and Viewpoint has worked hard to adapt accordingly. Not only has it embraced change; in some instances, Viewpoint has been trailblazing the modernisation of Sheltered Housing provision. In addition, the single Care Home concept has been adopted by Viewpoint. This ensures that as well as catering for the medical and physical needs of people living in Care Homes, residents experience an emphasis on the whole person, which enables them to continue to live life to the full.

Of course, none of this is possible without dedicated staff who are willing to learn and adapt to a changing organisation. In addition to establishing a Learning & Development culture, Viewpoint is now taking that a step further in taking forward a new policy of 'Work Place Learning'.

One of the main things I was keen to take into the future of Viewpoint as it develops, was its experience of the past. Having read the story I now appreciate the importance of this as well as the dedication of staff who have worked tirelessly over the years. I never had the pleasure of meeting Viewpoint's founder, Miss Cunningham, or her successor, Miss Ingham, and yet I feel that I know them so well. I have picked up a very important mantle from them and I am joined by 300 members of staff who strive to take their vision forward to the best of our abilities, embracing the future and whatever it has in store for us.

Margaret Wilkinson
April 2008

Preface

This isn't the first time that the story of Viewpoint has been told. I have benefited, in writing this history, from the accounts of others. The remarkable Miss Evelyn Ingham, the presiding spirit of Viewpoint for over forty years, was a founding member of the then Viewpoint Society and recorded her memories of the early days. They have been re-written, re-typed and re-worked on a number of occasions and provide the starting point for anyone wanting to understand the ethos of Viewpoint and the scale of its achievements.

To Miss Ingham's account should be added articles by Viewpoint's founder, Miss Jane Cunningham, and Norman Dunhill, Director from 1975 until 1992. Above all, I have been grateful for the work of Susan Maclennan. Her unpublished history of the organisation, written at the time of Viewpoint's 50th anniversary, has provided me with a starting point for many sections of this book. In particular, Chapter 9, dealing with Viewpoint's many ambitious fund raising initiatives, has been built upon Susan's own chapter on the subject, and Chapter 1 owes much to her observations arising from my first draft.

As well as drawing upon Viewpoint's archive of Minutes, cuttings and photos, it seemed important to hear from those who can speak of Viewpoint's past and present from direct experience. I am grateful to members of staff and to tenants and residents who were willing to share their stories and 'speak the truth in love.' Those who gave their time to be interviewed are included in the list of sources at the back of the book.

The advantage of speaking to individuals is that it allows the possibility of including stories, first-hand accounts, and abiding impressions that formal documents don't always convey. The disadvantage can be that some details are mis-remembered, others receive undue emphasis and events are inevitably described from particular perspectives. My task has been to strike a balance where required without stifling accounts that do so much to evoke the unique character of this organisation. Increasingly, I have felt my role to be that of a memory catcher. Memories, anecdotes, images – and even hearsay – all have their place in building a lasting impression of individuals and organisations. It became clear that if these were not drawn together as fully as possible now, much of the Viewpoint story would soon be lost irretrievably.

As well as taking the decision to weave first-hand accounts into the history where possible, it was also agreed that the story of this one, Edinburgh-based, Housing Association should be set within a wider context: the difficulties encountered by single women in society in the 1940s; the growing Housing Association movement throughout the UK; and evolving national housing and care policies. I've tried throughout not only to ask 'what, when, who and where' of Viewpoint but also 'why'. I have turned, on many occasions, to Richard Finlay's accessible history, *Modern Scotland*, in which he has undertaken the task of gathering together a good deal of pertinent statistical material. In addition, Peter Malpass's meticulous history of the development of Housing Associations and housing policy has been an essential reference point.

I am grateful to Joan Marshall, who first guided me through the treasure trove that is the Viewpoint archive and was also a reader of the book's first draft. Others who read parts or all of that draft, all with sensitivity and insight, were Norman Dunhill, George and Peggy Home, Susan Maclennan, Ian and Elisabeth Penman, and Margaret Wilkinson. Joan Marshall compiled the list of Chairs and senior officers in the appendix and, with Maureen Mack, also took time to sift through boxes and files of photos to find appropriate illustrations. My thanks, finally, to Ann Davies, whose careful proofing of the final text, accompanied by her customary wisdom and enthusiastic encouragement, were precisely what I required in order to bring this book to its final form. Naturally, any errors that remain are all my own.

As a student in Edinburgh in the mid-1980s, I trod a prescribed route between my flat and the university buildings. My knowledge of the city was, I now realise, strictly limited by a narrow way of life. I have been amazed to discover what Viewpoint was achieving virtually on my doorstep at that time, and the already remarkable niche it had carved out for itself in meeting the housing needs of older people in the city. Buildings I walked past every day were Viewpoint properties – outward signs of the Association's history and hopes. My understanding of Edinburgh is richer for having discovered something of Viewpoint's work and ethos, and the committed women who set it in motion. I'm grateful that there are those among the organisation's current staff and resident groups who were passionate enough to want to capture Viewpoint's history in written form.

Laurence Wareing

Chapter 1

Adding the personal touch – an introduction to Viewpoint

MEG, MOIRA AND DAN

I visit Inverard, Viewpoint's Sheltered Housing property close by Edinburgh's Royal Botanic Gardens. Like a good many of Viewpoint's older properties, Inverard was originally a large detached Edinburgh villa. Over time it has been extended and, at the time that Viewpoint bought the property from another local charity, a number of small, two-person bungalows were built within its grounds. Recently, further renovation has been undertaken – part of Viewpoint's policy of upgrading older-style bed-sits into more substantial and attractive two-room apartments. It has been a trying time for residents. They have had to adapt to changes that would be difficult for people of any age, but two of the three residents I am here to meet are, to my astonishment, approaching their 100th birthdays. Joint celebrations are already being planned.

I am taken into the lounge, where morning refreshments have been laid out in preparation for our conversation. This, I will discover, is quintessential Viewpoint hospitality. Tea and coffee are served in fine china, and plates are full with a range of home-baked cakes. Even for what is intended to be a research conversation there is a sense of things being done properly and of pleasure taken in adding the personal touch.

This, I will discover, is the Viewpoint way. In getting to know the organisation, I will hear about silver candlesticks on coffee morning tables, and sweeties placed on staff desks; of personalised thank you letters and of committees that agonise over how to address difficult matters concerning individual tenants. Above all, I will learn of the affection in which so many residents have been held. Time and again, a member of staff will say to me: 'Have you met so-and-so ... ?' or 'I remember Miss ... – she was a wonderful person.' It is clear that over the decades, whatever immediate difficulties have arisen, whatever frustrations staff and residents alike have encountered, Viewpoint never forgets who it is there for and why it is in the business of social housing and care.

On this particular visit, the residents I meet are vibrant and willing to offer strong opinions, but what is striking, even among this tiny group, is the variety of their backgrounds and reasons for moving to Inverard. Two have been living here for six years; the other since Inverard was acquired by Viewpoint in 1981. Dan Orr, a former senior banker, came because he already had close connections with Viewpoint. His wife had been a volunteer at the Association's successful Tanfield charity shop, and when she began to develop Alzheimer's disease they held out for a place with Viewpoint despite receiving offers from other Homes. Moira, the longest-serving of this group, has worked as a crèche manager on P&O cruise ships and as a secretary at St Thomas's Hospital in London. She has lived with Multiple Sclerosis for many years and found in Inverard a home suitable for her needs. Meg, meanwhile, can't tell me in any detail how she came to be living at Inverard, though it followed a stay in hospital. But on one thing she's absolutely clear: it's the best thing that has happened to her. 'I wouldn't exchange it except for a crown in heaven!'

SIXTY YEARS OF CARE

Viewpoint was founded in 1947, as former Viewpoint Housing Officer Susan Maclennan puts it, 'by women for women, to meet a previously unrecognised need. Many elderly and retiring women were living on very small fixed incomes and often coming out of tied accommodation. Often they were educated women who had been doing interesting wartime work and caring for elderly relatives. Many had remained single following the death of future husbands during the Great War. Now they were homeless. Their plight was not recognised in a society now recovering from the Second World War and where the aim was to create "Homes fit for Heroes"' (Chapter 2).

One of Scotland's first Housing Societies, Viewpoint responded in the first instance by purchasing properties that could be divided into bed-sits into which women could move with their own furniture (Chapter 4). These were pioneering developments that created a growing community of women drawn together not just by individual need, but through campaigning, social and fund raising activities. 'The trust and reciprocity that the women developed,' Susan argues, 'quickly raised the profile of the organisation and, very importantly, gave the members a sense of "ownership", which encouraged them to be actively involved.'

By building strategic relations within Edinburgh's

3

civic community, Viewpoint managed to acquire much of the prime property that has contributed to the organisation's character. Over time, a wide range of increasingly ambitious properties were developed (Chapters 7 & 8) and the provision, from the 1970s onwards, of Sheltered Housing (Chapter 10). General housing for a wider age-range has followed and, unusually for a housing organisation, Viewpoint developed in parallel with its housing projects a range of Residential Homes and care establishments (Chapter 8). This combination of housing *with* care – and the desire to provide continuity of care for its increasingly elderly community of tenants and residents – is undoubtedly what made Viewpoint unusual, at times unorthodox, and in many respects the pioneering organisation that it remains sixty years on.

Though Viewpoint has spread its wings, now offering services in Fife and the Lothians, for much of its life it was a distinctive Edinburgh institution. In developing properties in the locations it did, often with considerable architectural innovation and flair (Chapters 7 & 10), Viewpoint has made a physical contribution to the appearance of Scotland's capital that must be unique among the city's Housing Associations. Sometimes with self-confident panache, sometimes with self-effacing discretion, Viewpoint developments have been woven into Edinburgh's architectural heritage in a manner that entirely reflects the Association's traditional commitment to the needs of its citizens. But the provision of bricks and mortar was never Viewpoint's raison d'être; nor does its distinctive combination of housing with care facilities in itself explain the underlying ethos of the organisation.

I think of Meg, Moira and Dan – of their striking and individual personalities, and of their different needs – as I talk to former Viewpoint warden Marjory Sinclair about the very remarkable Miss Evelyn Ingham. For 40 years, Miss Ingham was both Secretary and inspiration to the organisation and to its staff, somewhat overshadowing the Association's founder, Miss Jane Cunningham. For many it is Miss Ingham's name that remains synonymous with all that Viewpoint stands for. For her, Marjory tells me (Chapter 7), 'it was always about seeing the person, not the problem'. It is this 'viewpoint' that most clearly encapsulates the ethos upon which the organisation was developed. It might be termed now a 'social model' of housing and care. Arguably, during the 1990s an increasing emphasis came to be laid on the 'problems' – not so much of individuals as of society at large. In order to acquire funding for development, Viewpoint had to respond more directly to the wider social issues that local and national government were endeavouring to address. However, it was precisely this need to follow government policy in the 1990s that led to Viewpoint's growing provision of housing for individuals returning to live in the community from long-term hospital care (Chapter 12). The Government's policy of Care in the Community would throw up its own problems but it might equally be said that Viewpoint's endeavours to welcome individuals into Homes rather than institutions was at one with its historic concern for the 'person, not the problem'.

Certainly, it is on the needs of the person that today's senior staff place priority. Sandra Brydon, currently Viewpoint's Housing Manager, insists that Viewpoint has always been good at 'putting the tenant at the centre' and speaks of the ways in which Viewpoint tenants have developed a growing role in the way their needs are represented to the organisation (Chapter 14). Likewise, Jane Douglas, until recently responsible for Viewpoint's Care Homes, sees an important distinction between homes and institutions: 'A Home where you live when you're older should be a home, not an institution. A hospital is an institution; a Home is a place where you come to live – not a place to come to die.'

There are basic needs, says Jane, which everyone expects to have met – to be washed, to be dressed, to be given food. But Viewpoint sets out to add to those basic needs and enhance every individual's quality of life. A meal organised in one or two sittings, for example, 'feels like a school dinner – institutionalised'. So, Viewpoint has been moving to a system where meals are served, as in a good hotel, between certain hours. Other details are important. There was a time when it was thought that table cloths might be a hazard – those living with dementia, it was argued, might pull them off. Nowadays, it is argued that residents who have dementia remain perfectly familiar with table cloths – so now they are being used again. Equally, glasses are used, not beakers; napkins, not bibs. Classical music might be playing in the background. Such details, says Jane, make meal times less institutional and encourage a healthy lifestyle. There are many who would also say that Viewpoint's willingness to re-embrace this 'social model' of care (and to adjust its staffing structures to reflect the move away from a 'medical model' of care) is pointing the way for others to follow. There is a pioneering spirit at the heart of

Viewpoint that has continually encouraged it to assess the needs of its residents and tenants and, in response, strike out on new and interesting paths.

In part, this re-emphasis on the experience of the individual is a response to documents produced by the Care Commission and the re-categorisation of all Nursing and Residential Homes as Care Homes. The consequence is that all Homes should now offer the social care you would expect within a Residential Home together with appropriate medical care when required. However, the approach that both Jane and Sandra describe is also one that Miss Ingham would have recognised. Most clearly, it informed the creation of Viewpoint's Guest House Homes and Residential Clubs (Chapter 8) but it was that same ethos of adding quality of life to the everyday existence of individuals which underpinned the development of all Viewpoint's early housing projects. It gave women what they needed when they needed it.

Given that it has always endeavoured to attend to the needs of the individual, it is perhaps unsurprising that Viewpoint has also been an organisation in which strong, committed individuals have made their mark. You cannot speak to Viewpoint stalwarts without quickly hearing of Miss Ingham, of the Viewpoint's founder, Miss Cunningham (Chapter 3), and of characterful men also – the imaginative fund raiser, Edward French (Chapter 9), and Viewpoint's two male directors to date, Norman Dunhill (Chapters 10 & 11) and Bob Duff (Chapter 12). These were 'charismatic individuals who,' comments Susan Maclennan, 'were not scared of bending rules, challenging the norms and thinking creatively to solve apparently insurmountable problems. Without the strength of personality of these individuals, one does wonder if such a shoestring business would have succeeded.'

But it did succeed. Viewpoint, like every other Housing Association, has faced its considerable ups and downs over the years. Yet, force of character inspired by dynamic leadership has driven the Association's growth, enriched its diversity and maintained its creativity. As a result, sixty years after its inception, Viewpoint can be proud of its position as Scotland's oldest existing Housing Association.

Chapter 2
A very particular need

On August 9, 1946, an article appeared in the *Christian Science Monitor* entitled 'Man is not homeless'. Published in America, the *Monitor* was, and remains, a well-regarded current affairs newspaper. The article is not attributed (the newspaper notes only that it has been written specifically for the *Monitor*) but it is deemed to be of sufficient interest to be printed both in English and Polish. In fact, the article's author was an Edinburgh woman, then in her late sixties, Miss Jane Cunningham.

'Man is not homeless' is primarily a reflection on the spiritual meaning of 'home'. However, Miss Cunningham's thoughts have arisen out of a very practical concern that has been troubling her for some time. She writes:

> *For many months, the writer felt keenly the trials of others unable to find homes, and so became interested in planning a much-needed housing project for her community. Hardship and overcrowding demanded that something be done and public-spirited people got together to form an organization which would help to remedy the desperate shortage...*[1]

Though Miss Cunningham doesn't name it, this is the earliest existing reference to what will become Viewpoint Housing Association. Specifically, her concern is for the large numbers of single women in Edinburgh, many of whom have worked in professional occupations but who have neither the means nor opportunity either to rent or purchase a home for their old age. In response to this very particular need, she has therefore recently instigated the fledgling housing enterprise to which her article alludes, clearly aware that the needs of these single women are not being covered by the provisions of the equally new and aspirational Welfare State.

Four years earlier, in 1942, the economist and social reformer William Beveridge had published a report commissioned by the Government. It had been designed to present a vision for how Britain might be rebuilt after the Second World War, and recommended ways of fighting the five 'Giant Evils' of 'Want, Disease, Ignorance, Squalor and Idleness.'

The Beveridge Report held out the promise of a more equal society to a nation then experiencing privations brought about by war. It spoke of economic wellbeing for every citizen regardless of age and means, and proposed the delivery of free universal health care and education. The report recommended social policies that would look after the needs of the most vulnerable. 'The resources of the state would be turned over to experts,' writes historian Richard Finlay, 'to construct the perfect society – or so the theory went.'[2]

Under Clement Atlee's Labour administration, the Welfare State envisaged by Beveridge began to take shape. Among a range of initiatives, the 1946 Health Service Act, overseen by Atlee's Minister for Health, Aneurin Bevan, promised a medical service free to all at the point of delivery. Additionally, because health and housing were seen as interrelated issues, Bevan was also responsible for two Housing Acts, in 1946 and 1949. Both were put forward to encourage council-led housing construction. To place these initiatives in perspective, it is worth pausing to assess briefly the housing situation in Britain as it had developed during the inter-war years of 1918 to 1939.

Housing was not a new issue for government. Politicians had begun to recognise it as a key issue following the First World War, though the impact of rapid demobilisation only exacerbated already deep-rooted problems. Richard Finlay describes a situation in which half the Scottish population at that time was living in one- or two-bedroomed houses. Overcrowding was accompanied by poor sanitation, which in turn led to disease and general bad health. Scotland's least overcrowded urban conurbation, Edinburgh, was only marginally better off than England's most overcrowded city, Sunderland.[3] Even before the war ended, a 1917 Royal Commission reported that it would take a quarter of a million new homes to relieve the situation in Scotland.

Faced with four million men being released from the services, Lloyd George promised 'homes fit for heroes'. As a response to general social unrest, to which an economic slump and the flu epidemics of 1918 and 1919 all contributed, the Government's scheme appears only to have scratched the surface of the nation's problems. Nevertheless, David Thomson concludes that the idea of homes for heroes, 'though not adequate to existing needs, established the notion that housing is a social problem, to be tackled on a national scale by getting houses built.'[4]

The inter-war years were not kind to Scotland. Richard Finlay's assessment is shocking:

> *The fact that the workshop of the Empire was flat broke and that the once mighty Scottish economy was on its knees seemed to reinforce the notion that Scotland was in a state of terminal decline ... In output, health, housing and a whole range of socio-economic statistics relating to standards of living, Scotland was lagging behind the rest of the United Kingdom. It was thought that Scotland would soon cease to exist as an identifiable nation.*[5]

In other words, just as in 1914, the economic prospects for Scotland in 1939 were gloomy, war or no war. For all that there was a 'change of national outlook and of popular resolve' following the Second World War, and a 'desire for fuller social justice, a lessening of class differences'[6], housing issues still loomed large on the political and social scene. In 1941, a War Damages Act had forbidden most new building and emphasised emergency repair work. This remained in force well after the end of the war. North of the border it was additionally recognised that the 'post-war reconstruction of Scotland would require more resource than the nation could provide by itself'.[7] There was acknowledgement, too, that in the face of fierce competition for materials, the greater damage to English housing and infrastructure by enemy action would further place Scotland at a disadvantage. George Home, who in the 1990s would become Chairman of Viewpoint, recalls being demobbed from the RAF and trying to find accommodation with his new wife, Peggy. The best they could afford was one room with a shared kitchen and bathroom. Choice, he says, was very limited.

In summary, building materials and labour were scarce, land for building was restricted, regulations were tight and funding was difficult. Moreover, voluntary housing organisations were especially hard hit, as Housing Policy expert Peter Malpass points out. The two world wars, he notes, 'are generally interpreted as giving housing policy a great boost, breaking down barriers that had previously appeared insurmountable.'

> *But an interest in voluntary housing organisations provides a different angle, for they experienced the immediate postwar periods as times of frustration and difficulty. From their point of view it was not until fifteen years after each war that their prospects really improved.*[8]

To this gloomy scenario we can add that the impact of housing shortages on women in particular was as significant in 1945 as it had been 25 years earlier.

Following the Great War, women had often been discharged from jobs in industry to make way for ex-service men. The aftermath of the Second World War made for a similar story. With the changing roles of women within society and greater access to educational opportunities, women had again filled the roles of absent men folk, but this time within the professions, teaching and the Civil Service as well as industry. Often, those single women with few family commitments could be sent anywhere in the country, many spending the war years in uncomfortable digs. Following the war, however, their lodgings and their temporary promotions had to be given up. Effectively homeless, these women added to the numbers of so-called 'professional women' over retirement age unable to apply for rented, let alone purchased, accommodation. If conditions were difficult for married couples, as George and Peggy Home's experience illustrates, then they were worse still for single women. As Norman Dunhill, Director of Viewpoint from 1974, puts it, 'women were not considered a "good risk" by Housing Societies', and with no domiciliary rights women were prohibited from putting their names on Local Authority housing waiting lists.

It was within this context – a national housing shortage, restrictions on new building and seemingly insuperable financial obstacles compounding the particular difficulties of single women – that Miss Cunningham, already approaching her 70s, decided to act. 'It's someone's fault, this lack of Housing', she wrote later in verses entitled simply 'Viewpoint Housing':

> *'Men in authority need rousing –*
> *Why don't they listen?' Everywhere*
> *Are plaints that border on despair.*
> *'I've waited for a house for years –*
> *And oh! the sins of profiteers!'*
>
> *'Too many people live alone –*
> *Selfish – so big a space to own!'*
> *'But sharing's harder than you think –*
> *No bath – one gas ring – one small sink?'*

•   •   •

'What can I do? I have no bricks,
Labour is short, cement is shorter,
And if I had the men and mortar
Restrictions hold me in a fix.'

Her first attempt to form a committee of prominent, public-spirited people who might help alleviate the problems faced by single women failed. For what reason is not clear. The 'hoped-for progress was not made,' she wrote in the *Christian Science Monitor*: 'doors that should have opened remained closed, and accomplishment seemed blocked in all directions. After a number of committee meetings, all action was indefinitely postponed.' Yet, by the time Miss Cunningham was writing her article in 1946, almost exactly a year after V-J Day and the end of the war, her plans had clearly made significant progress:

> *Finally, one who had been interested in the housing project proposed a plan on new lines which afforded fresh opportunity, and is still helpfully unfolding.*[9]

It is likely that this is a reference to Miss Cunningham's friend, the solicitor George Cheyne of Mill, Mcleod and Rose WS.[10] He had already helped her to buy a flat directly above his firm's offices in Edinburgh's Rutland Street, presumably applying on her behalf for the Building Society loan that she secured successfully.

The flat at number 27 Rutland Street had the typically spacious dimensions of a central Edinburgh tenement and Miss Cunningham, conscious that it was 'so big a space to own,' set about letting out rooms to other single women. This must have been the state of affairs that accorded her so much satisfaction when writing for the *Monitor*. Her plan was then to purchase another flat in order to let out rooms on a similar basis, though 'in humility and joy the lesson was learned that one must not hold tightly to "my house" and "my scheme", fancying oneself in the role of owner or benefactor.'[11] It seems that, at this point, George Cheyne, who would become the first male chairperson of Viewpoint, had proposed to Miss Cunningham that she form another committee with the express task of managing the leased properties.

So, in 1947, a second committee was established, this time of eight 'like-minded women' and a secretary, Miss Muriel Ellis, recently returned to Edinburgh from Geneva. The women were described as 'willing but without knowledge, but they were nevertheless prepared to roll up their sleeves and work.' They called themselves the Viewpoint Housing Society.

Housing Societies were not a new idea. The National Federation of Housing Societies, to which Viewpoint was affiliated, had been formed in 1935 with 35 founder members. Within the year, that number had risen to almost one hundred. Behind the Federation's work lay a long history of voluntary sector social housing, an area of enterprise at which Local Authorities arrived belatedly when the 1890 Housing of the Working Classes Act paved the way for them to become large scale providers of rented housing.[12] Of the voluntary organisations well-established by 1947, it is worth noting in particular the approach of the Octavia Hill Societies, a collection of relatively autonomous Housing Associations run along the lines of what Peter Malpass calls the Octavia Hill system. It was as much a social project as a system, based on middle class outreach to the deserving poor. Though targeted towards a different sector of society, its values are strongly echoed in Viewpoint's endeavours on behalf of business and professional women.

The founding members of the Viewpoint Housing Society are all named in the first Register of Members on February 11, 1947. Each of them has purchased one or more shares in the society at a cost of £1 each. Essentially, this was a fund raising mechanism. Others were also invited to take up membership of the society by purchasing 'share capital', a system that still holds today. Most of the earliest members were women, and the majority were single women who would have joined with a view to becoming a tenant in one of Viewpoint's houses. It was not required that shareholders should be tenants but it does appear that at this stage only shareholders were invited to take up Viewpoint's first available tenancies, a policy that would change over the years. Being a shareholder is no longer required in order to be a tenant or resident, though the two do often go hand in hand. Nowadays, some 85 per cent of current shareholders are tenants[13] and, now as then, shares are still sold at £1 each. They are non-refundable, accrue no interest and attract no dividend payments. A shareholder is, however, entitled to a vote at General Meetings.

We will return to the question of what kind of women were attracted to becoming members of Viewpoint (Chapter 8) but a glance at those who made up the first Viewpoint committee immediately indicates the range of skills that the 'like-minded women' brought to the enterprise. All but Miss Cunningham had an identifiable job or profession. The group includes a teacher, an architect, a hostel warden, an auditor's assistant (Miss Cunningham's neighbour in Rutland Street, Mrs Elizabeth Winter) and a housing manager. Miss Cunningham's own sister, Elizabeth, is listed. She was a nurse and, at that point, the majority share holder having purchased one hundred shares. Also listed among this first group are Miss Ann Evelyn Ingham ('Artist'), who would become the organisation's driving inspiration, and the Secretary, Miss Ellis – who ensures that she is registered as Secretary '*and Manager*' of Viewpoint. She took on this role for an honorarium only, which was all that Viewpoint could pay.

In his history of the National Housing Federation, *Turning Hopes into Homes*, James Tickell notes that 'the original identity of social housing, going back over a thousand years, is clearly philanthropic, charitable and voluntary'.

> *Altruism, religion, civic duty all played a part in the founding of early housing bodies ... Charity was seen as a civic duty, and played a fundamental role in mitigating the worst effects of social injustice and inequality.*[14]

It's a description that undoubtedly captures the motivations of Viewpoint's founder members, of whom Miss Elizabeth Russell Cockburn provides a striking example. A future chairperson of Viewpoint (1963–77), Miss Cockburn was born in 1893. She trained as a teacher, holding a position in the East End of London before returning to Edinburgh, where she taught in various schools including Leith Academy and the nearby Links

Place School. According to notes for an obituary, Miss Cockburn gained a qualification in horticulture and ran school allotments. The writer notes that this activity not only offered children a new experience and pleasure but it also supplemented school funds from the sale of produce. Given the important roles that both practical resourcefulness and fund raising were to play in the development of Viewpoint, it would appear that Elizabeth Cockburn was tailor-made for membership of its managing committee.

However, Miss Cockburn also brought to Viewpoint a campaigning spirit. She was already active in local politics and known as a public speaker, particularly on behalf of the Women's Pension League – a campaign for single women to receive a pension from the age of 55. Writing to the *Edinburgh Evening News* in August 1936, she declares:

> *We are told that the annual expenditure required to finance these pensions would build a battleship. That argument leaves us cold. We estimate ourselves more precious to the country than one battleship and our value will not depreciate.*

She goes on to list the injustices that single women have to put up with. Women are, she argues, still worth less to the labour market, though indispensable to it; and, in spite of lower pay, they have to contribute a full share of Income Tax. Furthermore, she says, men get a better deal out of the Health Insurance system because their insurance carries benefits for widows and children also.

It's hardly surprising that Miss Cockburn was willing

to become involved in an organisation designed, within its specific sphere of interest, to offer better opportunities for women. However, her broader concern for the welfare of single women meant that she also brought existing experience of housing issues to Viewpoint. In her capacity as a member of the Pension League she had contributed an article (possibly during the inter-war period) to 'Eve's Circle'. This was a regular column in the *Edinburgh Evening News* featuring women's issues and initiatives – and one that became something of an advocate for Viewpoint's endeavours during the organisation's early years. Here, Elizabeth Cockburn describes a recent visit to London and, albeit with reference exclusively to women of below retirement age, echoes precisely the concerns that Miss Cunningham wished to address.

> *Nowadays the labour market depends very largely on the services of single women, and still very little consideration is given to their problem of where to stay at an economic rent.*
>
> *During a recent visit to London I was amazed at the provision made for their accommodation. Many of the large stores, employing much female labour, have now a living-in system which is generous and even luxurious.*

She reports her impressions of one complex of 500 furnished bedrooms with communal areas ('it was a revelation to a Scot to see such an up-to-date provision') and describes in detail another housing initiative built specifically for women and comprising one and two-apartment flats built to high specification. 'The most enviable thing was the provision of constant hot water...':

*I just wished I could have transported them to Edinburgh,
where the demand is so very great and the response to this
clamant need so very poor.*

In their time, argues James Tickell, the early Housing
Associations 'were at the leading edge of progressive
social change.'[15] Certainly, many 'tended to be formed
from those among the "great and the good" who were
socially concerned', but Viewpoint appears to have
brought an unusually wide range of backgrounds to its
first committee – as well as the relevant knowledge and
experience of women such as Elizabeth Cockburn. They
offered, above all, an extraordinary level of can-do
commitment, and this (like most other such
independent housing organisations) in the face of very
limited access to public funds and no coherent
regulatory structures.[16]

Miss Ingham later recalled the difficulties that the
women had in raising money for the first Viewpoint
house, indicating that the income raised by selling shares
barely began to bring in what was required. 'Neither
building society nor Local Authority would help an
untried organisation. It was only due to the kindness of
our lawyers and to friends that some money was gathered
for the purchase of the first house.'

At a cost of £1,100, the property in question was a
main door flat located at 9 Warrender Park Crescent,
close by the green and leafy expanse in Edinburgh
known as The Meadows. In making the purchase, the
Committee unwittingly acquired, also, the former owner

and his invalid wife as caretakers. The ground floor and basement apartment contained just seven rooms and would demand shared use of a communal kitchen and bathroom. It was to be called Anne House.

Miss Cunningham's housing project was unfolding at last. Anne House would replicate her own small-scale response to the needs of single women already operating at 28 Rutland Street. By modern standards, the arrangements at Anne House and its immediate successors could offer only what Norman Dunhill describes as 'inferior accommodation' – bed-sits with shared cooking facilities. Nevertheless, given the post-war context in which Viewpoint was operating and the financial limitations imposed on women, this was a pragmatic and forthright first step. The committee would surely have been astonished to realise where that step would lead over the next sixty years – how society's needs and expectations would change and how diverse social housing opportunities would become.

But before considering that journey, it's worth pausing to ask about Miss Cunningham herself. If, as James Tickell says, altruism, religion and civic duty were shared characteristics that led to the founding of many early Housing Associations, what in particular motivated Jane Cunningham? What was it that led her, at the age of 68 and with apparently few personal resources, to recruit these 'like-minded women' and embark upon an enterprise that might have seemed daunting to a woman half her age?

Chapter 3
Miss Cunningham

Still sitting in the Viewpoint offices in South Oswald Road, Edinburgh, is an early and very heavy Remington standard typewriter. With its sturdy metal cover, like a small, squat coal scuttle, it sports the Remington motto: 'To save time is to lengthen life'. Almost certainly, it once belonged to Viewpoint's founder, Miss Jane Cunningham. She once described typing as 'my one wage-earning accomplishment' and photos of her in later life typically show her, smart and trim and with a focused demeanour, bent towards her typewriter. Her wry observation is at one with a consistently modest self-assessment of her achievements, and the ability to type certainly complemented her ambitions as a writer. However, it also serves to highlight how little we actually know about the woman who established Scotland's longest-serving Housing Association.

Few of Miss Cunningham's personal documents remain in the Viewpoint archives, though those that do suggest a woman who liked to record her memories accurately. One photo shows her in 1962, aged 83, preparing to take the sleeper train from London Euston to Stranraer. She carries her umbrella 'bought in 1898' and holds a rose sent by 'Edwin ... which lasted over a week'. Who Edwin was, and why he gave her a single rose remains for us an attractive little mystery. The photo indicates simply that, well into her final years, Miss Cunningham was a woman who maintained her independence and had close friends.

What we have of Miss Cunningham's type-written 'Autobiography' extends only into her young womanhood, petering out once she crosses the Channel with her father to live in Italy. We don't know what her politics were and can't be absolutely certain about her religious affiliation. How she supported herself, beyond receiving sporadic payments for articles or royalties (such as they were) for her novels, is not at all clear. Nor does she write in any overt way about Viewpoint itself, despite the organisation dominating most of the last two decades of her life.

Even Miss Cunningham's name requires a light question mark to be placed over it. In the first Viewpoint Register of Members, her name is entered as Miss *Jean* Margaret Munro Cunningham (occupation unspecified), despite being referred to in all other documents – including on the title pages of her two published novels – as *Jane*. Since the names of all first eight members of the Society were entered in a single hand, probably by the Secretary, Muriel Ellis, it is likely that the use of 'Jean' (albeit the Scottish version of Jane) is an uncorrected if somewhat surprising error. Not that Miss Cunningham would often have been referred to in later life by her first name. In keeping with the custom of the time, at least among the middle classes, the respectable ladies of Viewpoint hid their first names behind a discreet veil of propriety.

Any account of Miss Cunningham's life, therefore, is going to be limited. Yet, it is worth pursuing so far as one can in order to gain some understanding of the values that underpinned her early vision for a Housing Society. What persuaded her to act in the way that she did and – in the absence of any 'Mission Statement' – what did she think Viewpoint stood for?

She was born on July 22, 1879, at 7 Brandon Street, on the edge of Edinburgh's New Town, the third daughter of a Free Church minister, the Revd Dr John G Cunningham, and his wife Margaret. The Anglo-Zulu war, which had been fought since the beginning of the year, had come to a conclusion just three weeks earlier. In the dying days of the same year, Scotland would witness the shocking Tay Bridge rail disaster. That year in Edinburgh, the young Robert Louis Stevenson (born just a short walk away from Dr Cunningham's manse) published what would be his first enduring work, *Travels with a Donkey in Cevennes*.

This was a time of some considerable social change. Under Benjamin Disraeli and the Conservatives, the Climbing Boys Act had recently reinforced the prohibition against employing juvenile chimney sweeps. In the same year, 1875, the Public Health Act laid down in detail what Local Authorities had to do in order to promote public health. They had to ensure, for example, that there was an adequate running water supply, drainage and sewage disposal. Also in that year, and with a bearing on the context in which the evolving Viewpoint Housing Society would find itself operating, the Artisans Dwelling Act gave Local Authorities the power to destroy slums and replace them with modern, healthy housing. However, this initiative was presented in the form of voluntary powers rather than as a compulsory order.

For women, too, times were changing. It was twelve years since the Scottish Women's Suffrage Society had held meetings for the first time. In 1882, three years after Jane was born, married women would gain the right to own property – though not, as we have already noted, single women. The pressure for universal women's suffrage would mount during Jane's lifetime, given a boost by the vital work undertaken by women during the First World War. In Edinburgh, Dr Elsie Inglis was one of those women changing public perception of women's rights and of what they could achieve. It seems likely that Jane (whose own sister Elizabeth aspired to be a doctor) would have become aware of Dr Inglis' work in providing medical care for women and, in 1914, her determination to support the war effort by working with the army in Europe. Yet, as broadcaster Jenni Murray writes of her own grandmother, born in the same year that Elsie Inglis opened a small hospital in Edinburgh's George Square:

> *A girl born in 1899 ... had little chance of evading the role that was considered her destiny – to marry young, stay home and raise a family ... only the privileged few, whose fathers or husbands were enlightened enough to permit it, got a foot on the ladder of opportunity.*[17]

Jane Cunningham never married and had to make her own opportunities, but she was not without encouragement from her father. A successful student and accomplished linguist, Dr Cunningham was inducted in 1859 into the small country charge of Lochwinnoch in present-day Renfrewshire. He held that charge for sixteen years before moving to Edinburgh in 1876 to become a minister at St Luke's Free Church, Young Street, alongside the Revd Alexander Moody Stuart.[18] In 1891, St Luke's united with the Tolbooth Church to become the Queen Street congregation – unique in Free Church history in boasting a team of four ministers.[19]

The year after the move to Edinburgh, Jane was born. 'I was plain, unwholesome-looking and morbid,' she writes, and was nick-named by her cousin 'The Frog.' (This didn't dim her affection for Cousin William whom she still found 'delightful.') The family moved in 1885 to 15 Saxe Coburg Place, with its central private gardens in which the children played while Jane observed from a distance.

> *I had no spirit to play, and was afraid of other children. When I went into the garden in the middle of the square, someone carried a little chair for me, on which I sat, with gloves on, and wished it was time to go home.*[20]

In another article submitted to *The Christian Science Monitor* ('An Edinburgh Citizen remembers', dated August 11, 1952), she recalls 'hoky-poky', clove balls and other sweets on sale outside her nursery window, noting that 'one did not buy from barrows in those far off days.'

In 1888, the family moved again, this time to Queen Street, at the heart of Dr Cunningham's central Edinburgh parish. In the same *Monitor* article, Jane writes of horse-drawn vehicles and of Dr Joseph Bell ('Dr Joe'), the model for Conan Doyle's Sherlock Holmes, riding a smart, horse-drawn 'Victoria' carriage and 'wearing a tall hat, bolt upright with a fur rug over his knees.' Of this same area also she comments:

*Now that Scottish Nationalism is much talked of, it may
be worth recalling that in earlier days we were contented
in an atmosphere of placid Hanoverian loyalty. Nobody
objected to our new Town streets bearing such names as
commemorate English notables ...*[21]

Jane was considered a delicate child and was educated for
the most part at home where she recalls being influenced
by her mother's love of history, music, French and Italian.
With her brothers and sisters, she also enjoyed the
classics, music and acting. From the age of seven, she was
writing stories and her lively imagination was fuelled still
further by summer vacations to her grandmother's home
near Stranraer, in an area of Scotland that would feature
significantly in her later writing. Here she would play
with her Aunt Lizzie who, in the guise of 'Tom', 'married'
the young Jane and maintained the fanciful habit of
addressing her as 'Beloved wife' until her death in 1920.

Already, Jane was exhibiting characteristics that one
can imagine were strengthened in later life, among them
an enthusiasm for taking the lead. In Stranraer, at Jane's
request, Aunt Lizzie (another 'Miss Cunningham')
arranged to bring together a small weekly gathering for
Bible Class, which Jane and her friend Ivy led: a first,
instance, perhaps, of persuading others to act on her
behalf. A strong sense of moral propriety is also evident.
She began producing her own revised edition of
Shakespeare, 'substituting words of my own for anything
which I thought should not be there.'

In 1894, when Jane was fifteen, her mother died, and
three years later her eldest sister also died, following a
nine-month illness. 'I cannot write about it,' is all that she

can bring herself to say in her autobiography. As a result of these changes in their circumstances, Jane's second sister, Elizabeth had to give up her medical studies in order to take care of the house and assist their father in congregational work. However, while on a trip to Hungary, John Cunningham suffered an unspecified accident which led to poisoning in his leg and a series of serious operations. It was at this time that Jane taught herself to type in order to assist her father who had been commissioned to write a series of Bible notes for the Edinburgh publisher, Thomas Nelson.

Dr Cunningham seems never to have fully recovered from his illness. He was left weak and lame and, apparently for health reasons, in 1902 he took up the work of the 'Scotch' Chaplaincy at San Remo on the Riviera. Now aged 24, Jane joined him there, allowing Elizabeth to return to London in order to continue her studies in 'massage and medical electricity'. Her entry as one of the founding committee members of the Viewpoint Housing Society describes her as a nurse, suggesting that though Elizabeth was unable to complete her training to become a doctor, she was able to develop in other ways her hoped-for career within the medical profession.

Given her upbringing, it is hardly surprising that religious conviction contributed to Jane Cunningham's motivations for founding Viewpoint. Her 1946 article for *The Christian Science Monitor*, though alluding to the beginnings of the Society, is essentially a testimony to spiritual guidance and religious conviction. Speaking of the hurdles she had encountered in establishing a committee, she argues that it was by reflecting on her faith that she found a way forward:

Our thinking determines our environment, and as it grows in faith, love, purity and spiritual power, it expands our sphere of action ... When the writer had taken a definite mental stand for beginning with God and His perfect creation, when earnest prayer had purified personal desire and illumined human thinking, it was not long before interesting developments appeared.[22]

What may be surprising, though, is Miss Cunningham's apparent change of loyalties from the Free Church Presbyterianism of her upbringing to the tenets of Christian Science, a denomination founded in America by Mary Baker Eddy. It is generally assumed that Jane Cunningham became a Christian Scientist in later life. Evidence for this is relatively slim but does support the assertion. Her later articles were written for *The Christian Science Monitor* and her colleague at Viewpoint, Evelyn Ingham, was a practising Christian Scientist (as were at least two other early members of Viewpoint[23]). Whether the two ladies met through this shared commitment or whether Jane Cunningham was influenced by her friendship with Miss Ingham, we don't know. However, the 1946 article, 'Man is not Homeless', shows evidence that Miss Cunningham had read Mary Baker Eddy's *Science and Health with Key to the Scriptures* (the founding document of the denomination) and she clearly states that she reflected on her initial failure to establish a working group 'in the light of Christian Science.' Nevertheless, Viewpoint was not established as a Christian organisation and from Jane Cunningham's other writings it becomes evident that her motivations were not solely derived from religious commitment.

Jane had pursued literary ambitions for nearly all her life and recalls that she was already writing stories at the age of seven. As a teenager she wrote a tale that she ambitiously titled *Self-Will and Destiny*.

> *Owing chiefly to my father being so well known, the book was for a few weeks in most of the booksellers' windows. I used to look in at it almost daily, pretending I was absorbed by something else.*[24]

She won a number of writing competitions on religious topics: for the Free Church 'Welfare of Youth' competition, essays on Pascal and the Maccabees; for the Religious Tract Society, a story dealing with 'present-day aspects of the conflict with Sacerdotalism', which won her £50. At her father's suggestion, Jane also took on the commitment of writing a monthly letter to an American paper, The Presbyterian Banner, giving news of Scottish affairs and church life.

This interest in writing had been encouraged early by her father, who would drop her off at the Edinburgh Subscription Library on George Street while he was attending meetings. It was a place she loved, with 'no filing system; no red tape; no barrier' – and 'no ladies, so far as I remember'.[25] She portrays herself as a girl aged ten and reminiscent of Roald Dahl's book-loving Matilda, ensconced on the floor between leather armchairs and spiral staircases, devouring tales of chivalry and especially the work of Thackeray's daughter, Mrs Richmond Ritchie.

A passion for history, generously tinted with a romantic hue that one reviewer (with equal generosity) compared with Sir Walter Scott, was fully exploited in Jane Cunningham's two published novels. *The Baker's Window* (really a series of related short stories and a concluding play) was published in 1933, when Jane was 54. Its sequel, *Clearance*, followed the next year. *The Baker's Window* deals with tales and legends connected with an aristocratic family, the Eliots of Landrick, who hail from Jane's much loved Galloway. Fanciful and pious by turns, the book conjures up druids and crusaders and a love affair between the Earl's granddaughter and Duncan Ross, the hunchback son of a local pub landlord. *Clearance* ranges further afield, from a Scottish country manse to Harley Street in London. Its heroine is the daughter of a Free Church minister. It was advertised by *The Book Tag* as 'an interesting and rather curious piece of writing which should please those who require a casual but intriguing narrative.' A review printed in *The Glasgow Bulletin* is less evasive, describing the book as 'not so much a novel as an introduction to a rather complicated but pleasant Scots 19th century family ... There is of course a religious or philosophical purpose behind Miss Cunningham's story – a purpose which does not always make for clarity of narration.'

Miss Cunningham's 'religious or philosophical purpose' did find some focus however, in the section of *The Baker's Window* titled 'The Monument.' It tells of how Duncan Ross travels to Edinburgh and comes into contact with Thomas Muir, the real-life 18th century campaigner for political reform and the extension of the franchise to secure representation of the industrial classes. Muir is depicted distributing copies of Thomas Paine's radical pamphlet, *The Rights of Man*, which explored ideas of liberty and human equality. Muir and his fellow-activists were charged with sedition and transported to Australia. In 1845, a 90-foot high obelisk was constructed to their memory in Calton Old Burial Ground in Edinburgh. This section of Miss Cunningham's book was based on a booklet that she had already written, describing the origins of the monument – 'a masterly description of the days when men of conviction were fighting for the rights of men', wrote the *Ardrossan and Saltcoats Herald.*

Muir's story was one that struck a chord with Jane Cunningham. In 1961 she re-worked the material from 'The Monument' for a play (also set on the Galloway coast) called *Behold the Mountain.* This time a story of liberty, equality and fraternity is told to a group of 'international young people banded together to do a piece of reconstruction work' in a remote corner of Wigtownshire. Without wishing to make great claims for its literary merit, arguably the setting and the themes of this play are emblematic of Jane Cunningham's approach to life in general. Statements concerning equality, democracy and the rights of the needy crop up regularly in her writing – as does an insistence on banding together to do something about it.

It is likely, too, that Jane had an admiration for the American way of doing things. Her paternal grandfather, the Revd Robert Cunningham, had been vice-president of Lafayette College in Pennsylvania between 1837 and 1839, and her father had often travelled to the United States on church business. As a child, Jane would have met American friends who came as guests to the family home. It was surely no coincidence that when, following the success of Viewpoint, she decided to form a second Housing Association, the name chosen for it was borrowed from President Roosevelt's famous 1941 speech, 'The Four Freedoms'. Two of those freedoms in particular – freedom from want and freedom from fear – must have resonated strongly with Miss Cunningham as she undertook her work for single women. Their rights and 'freedom', at least in relation to housing in post-war Scotland, were low down the political and social priority list.

If religious sentiments underpin much of Miss Cunningham's thought, then it is a kind of practical religion that supports and works for equal rights. In the absence of any other evidence, is it too fanciful to believe that fundamentally this was what Viewpoint stood for? Was the 'viewpoint' that informed the first committee's ambitions – of equal rights for single women and the need for housing opportunities – but one aspect of their broader social commitments?

Miss Cunningham pursued a pragmatic response to a particular need, and she recognised that it was the kind of cause that could draw together the skills and energies of a wide range of like-minded volunteers, whether religiously inclined or not. Blending religious imagery with a deep-rooted respect for anyone who endeavours to make life better for others, she wrote in 1963:

Now here is the surprising fact that's worth considering. A great many people care. Beginning with the Welfare State, there are Societies, guidance Councils, psychiatrists, doctors, nurses, clergy and hundreds of philanthropic individuals daily engaged in caring for life's poor straying sheep. People, many not outwardly religious, giving tirelessly, unselfishly, of their knowledge, their patience, their energy, their money. Advisers, leaders, voluntary secretaries. A multitude, not recognisable as the angelic host, but all eagerly wanting to be not just other sheep, but shepherds ... It is one thing, in an emergency to do some splendidly unselfish act to save another, but it is a still greater achievement to toil through long years for people who may never express gratitude.[26]

Chapter 4
The alphabet houses

Quite apart from the specific financial barriers and practical difficulties faced by the first Viewpoint committee, the year in which the society was founded was a tough one for Britain as a whole. The winter of 1947 was especially harsh. Icebergs were reported off the Norfolk coast and the sea froze at Margate. Even in London temperatures dropped to as low as minus nine degrees centigrade and much of the country ground to a halt. By February, the related power crisis had become so grave that factories were being closed and, at home, people went to bed to keep warm in the day. As the year progressed, the austerity that had characterised the war years continued. In June the weekly milk allowance was reduced to two and a half pints and newspapers were restricted to just four pages each. By September, meat rationing had been cut once more and motoring for pleasure was banned.[27]

Within this bleak context, there were occasional events that gave cause for celebration. While the delivery of independence to India in August evoked mixed feelings, almost universal rejoicing greeted the marriage, on November 20, of HRH Princess Elizabeth and Lieutenant Philip Mountbatten, recently titled the Duke of Edinburgh. It was, wrote the *Manchester Guardian*, a 'first postwar sight of pageantry and colour', but one which nevertheless took some account of the prevailing economic conditions.[28] The Princess received the Government's standard extra 200 clothing coupons, allowed to all brides, but also 25 dresses from the New York Institute of Dress Designers (twenty of which were passed on to other brides getting married at the same time). The wedding breakfast, however, was limited to just 150 guests and three courses, with partridge as a main dish since it was not rationed.[29]

Earlier in the year, there had been another significant public event, this time in Scotland. On August 24, the first Edinburgh International Festival opened under the direction of the Viennese opera impresario, Rudolf Bing. Its founders aimed to enliven and enrich the cultural life of Europe, Britain and Scotland and to 'provide a platform for the flowering of the human spirit'[30] – an aspiration with which one can imagine that members of the Viewpoint committee (not least the artistically-inclined Miss Ingham) would have concurred.

Meanwhile, plans for the new Housing Society were progressing. Members were being added to the Register rapidly, including Viewpoint's first male members. George Duguid Cheyne, the society's supportive lawyer, was registered as a member on March 13 and, one month later, an Advocate, Mr J J Cunningham – though whether this was Miss Cunningham's elder brother, we do not know. Other men who purchased shares in the early days of Viewpoint would include an optician, a joiner, a retired schoolmaster and an 'asphalt sheeter' – suggesting, perhaps that the organisation attracted interest from a wider social range than one might have expected.

Quite how fast membership grew after the initial

rush of names is difficult to gauge. When Viewpoint's first property was opened in January 1948, the *Edinburgh Evening Dispatch* reported a figure of around 150 members. Certainly, there were far more prospective tenants on the waiting list for the new rooms than Anne House or its immediate successors could possibly accommodate. It was a scenario that would continue for many years. However, since dates on which shares were purchased are not always recorded, it is difficult to be precise about the exact state of the society's membership at this time. What we can be surer about is that by the preceding autumn of 1947, Viewpoint was one of twenty Housing Societies in Scotland as defined by the 1935 Housing Act. It was this Act that had introduced the legal concept of a 'housing society'. In that same year, the National Housing Federation had been founded as the 'National Federation of Housing Societies', a body to which Viewpoint was affiliated.

In the autumn of 1947, Miss Merrylees of the NFHS addressed a conference called by the Edinburgh Branch of the National Council of Women and the Edinburgh Women Citizens Association. Miss Cunningham was also among the speakers. An un-attributed newspaper report notes that there was a call for more housing to be made available to middle income groups. Local Authorities, it was declared, were struggling to house people with young families and, in a statement that mirrors remarkably the situation in Scotland sixty years on, the reporter continues:

The case was quoted of young couples faced with a problem of buying houses at much inflated prices, so that they were millstones round their necks for years, yet there were not houses for rent, and no alternative.[31]

Miss Merrylees argued that 'it seemed the time for voluntary organisations to get together to help the minority groups', among them single and older people. The following January, the *Edinburgh Evening News* concurred, saying that very little provision was being made in Edinburgh in the way of 'bachelor flats', which were envisaged as:

> *blocks of small flats designed for single professional women who have neither time nor money to run a whole house but who wish to have an establishment of their own where they can entertain friends without fear of disturbing their neighbours.*[32]

At the 1947 conference, Miss Merrylees reported that there was no government subsidy available for 'reconditioning' properties but since Local Authorities could make grants it was advisable, she said, to 'keep in with them'. The news reporter wrote:

> *They must look favourably at [reconditioning] for it was economical of labour and material, and stepped up accommodation for one family to meet the needs of several.*

This, of course, was precisely Viewpoint's approach, though the example cited on this occasion is of the Housing Committee of Newcastle and Tyneside branch of the National Council of Women. It had raised money, secured the co-operation of other women's organisations, bought a house and adapted it for elderly retired women of the business and professional classes with an income of not more than £3 a week. Rents, which the Committee hoped to reduce in time, were set at between 12/6 and £1 a week. Likewise, Viewpoint's intention would be 'to keep rents as moderate as is compatible with a sound economic base'.

Miss Cunningham also had her eye on Glasgow Corporation's policy of providing flats for single women (in what was an exception to Miss Merrylees' general picture). A newspaper cutting from around this time reports the Corporation's plans for a scheme within the Pollok housing estate – a four-storey block containing 61 flats, 'each consisting of living-room with bedroom, with kitchen and bathroom accommodation'. It would be some while before Viewpoint was in a position to offer accommodation anywhere near so spacious, though according to the *Edinburgh Evening News*, Viewpoint had ambitions in that direction even before Anne House was opened: 'some of the members have been to London and Sweden and seen just what can be done in this way'. For the moment, however, the only option was to buy and adapt.

Anne House was opened for viewing on January 15, 1948. An announcement had gone out a month earlier:

TO ALL MEMBERS:
You will be glad to know that your Committee of Management has made a beginning by acquiring the Society's first house – No.9, Warrender Park Crescent, in which there will be accommodation for some seven tenants.

> *You are invited to a Bring and Buy Sale there on January 15th, 1948, from 3 to 7pm. This will help our funds.*
>
> *Any Member who would like to be considered for atenancy in this house must send in her name to the Secretary between the 16th and 20th January, inclusive, stating definitely for which room she is making application.*

One newspaper headline hailed it as 'Women's Solution to City Housing Problem'. Its seven rooms were laid out over the ground and basement floors of the tenement building and the property was freshly painted and decorated throughout. The seven rooms were of varying sizes and tenants shared a communal kitchen and one 'antique bathroom ventilating on to a shaft but without daylight'. 'We also had rabbit hutches', recalled Miss Ingham. 'At least that's what they looked like but they were really larders, each with its own padlock'.

The hot and cold water system in one tenant's room, reads another report, 'was completely hidden from view by a cream-coloured fitment, resembling a dressing table, which blended perfectly with the colour scheme and looked quite innocent of playing a double act!' The rooms were unfurnished, allowing residents to bring their own furniture, and rents were set at between 15 and 28 shillings a week according to the size of the room. This rate included the cost of amenities and the services of a live-in caretaker.

The viewing day itself served a number of purposes, as it would with the opening of successive properties. Primarily it was an opportunity for those who had purchased shares in the Society to look at rooms that they might be interested in renting. One report has some fun with the comments of prospective tenants:

> *'Now don't you take the room I'm after.' 'No, I'm going for the one in the basement.' 'Here's a room for 16s a week facing the front, but the one at the back for 26s a week is bigger.'*[33]

If the dialogue is not unrealistic, perhaps it fails to convey the rare opportunity on offer here and what having any of the seven rooms might mean to the women in question. After all, the enterprise had been funded, as one report put it, 'almost wholly by those who know what it is to be without the desired type of accommodation.' After interested women had made their application to the Society, tenants would then be chosen by ballot. This, Miss Cunningham told the *Evening Dispatch*, was the fairest method and the reason why the Committee had decided to open the house for viewing.

There were other side-benefits too. The event had been advertised as a reminder to members of the Viewpoint Housing Society Limited of a 'Bring and Buy Sale.' Each successive House viewing would include a sale designed to raise funds to cover incidental expenses and for 'added extras' within the house. These sales were the forerunners of Viewpoint's later fund raising enterprises. The other side-benefit was publicity, aided on this occasion by the presence of the Lady Provost, Miss Rodney Murray, who opened Anne House formally. She is pictured in one photograph 'inspecting kitchen arrangements,' an image that to today's eyes might have an air of condescending patronage about it – an impression unfortunately supported by the presumably unintended irony in her speech:

> *This is a scheme planned by women for women and, as a*
> *woman's place is in the home, I am very glad to have the*
> *opportunity of doing anything at all to help some business*
> *women to have a home of their own.*

The comments hardly do justice to Miss Murray's genuine concern for the housing welfare of women in the city. In opening Anne House she said that the majority of correspondence that reached her at the City Chambers dealt with housing problems. Recently, she had revived the 'Lady Provost's Committee', designed to draw women into practical action for the welfare of Scotland's capital, and had made special mention of the 'initiative and courage' of women like Miss Cunningham. She regarded it as 'a very hopeful sign' that a project such as Viewpoint should be undertaken 'in spite of present difficulties and discouragement.'[34]

The project was expanded later in 1948 when two further houses were acquired. Bridget House (at 5 Northumberland Street) and Charlotte House (203 Newhaven Road) continued another tradition inaugurated by Anne House – the alphabetical naming of properties. Suggestions for names were voted upon by the Committee, with the final selection often being the first name of one of the Society's members. It was a system that would continue for eight properties in total, concluding with the naming of Hester House (also in Northumberland Street) in 1952.

Both opening for viewing on the same day, Saturday September 4, Bridget House offered rooms for eight women (again all sharing a single kitchen) and Charlotte House had accommodation for twelve women. Share capital and personal investments in loan stock made up some of the purchase price but Miss Ingham recorded that Bridget House was bought with a Building Society loan – 'so that was a great relief':

> *but building restrictions were still with us, and no one was allowed to spend more than £300 on repairs – and although this was later increased to £600 it still only allowed minor roof repairs or partial re-wiring.*

Rents at Bridget House ranged from 17s 6d to 35s a week, and at Charlotte House from 15s to 26s. The rooms in both houses were considered 'spacious'.

The special guest at the Bridget House viewing was the Countess of Elgin, a member of the Fife County Council Housing Committee. She confirmed the continuing necessity of enterprises such as Viewpoint, saying that 'she knew well that overcrowding and living in sub-let rooms was the sad lot of so many just now. Local Authorities were doing their utmost to rehouse families but the single woman often had to fend for herself'.[35]

As expectations shifted, Anne, Bridget and Charlotte Houses would eventually be considered inadequate for appropriate single living. From the mid 1970s onwards, they would be sold off – but for the moment they were a welcome contribution to the limited mix of available housing in Edinburgh. Indeed, by September 1948,

Viewpoint's membership was running to 250 members. With only 27 rooms so far made available to members, the committee made the decision to close the membership list for the time being.

Visiting Anne House shortly after it had been opened, a reporter described being entertained by one of the first tenants, who appeared quite satisfied with the living arrangements.

> *The fact that the kitchen of the house, though well equipped with cookers and gas rings, is shared by eight women has been a subject of criticism in some quarters. Up till now, however, its sharing has created no difficulties and not a single instance of women falling over each other in a frantic rush to be first at the cooker has been recorded! True, all the residents have not yet arrived, but so pleasant is the atmosphere of the house that my hostess was quite optimistic about its future.*[36]

Rather soon, such rosy optimism would hit the harder realities of communal living, but for now Viewpoint was up and running and, crucially, beginning to meet the very particular need that had been identified by Miss Cunningham.

Chapter 5
So much so cheaply

From Viewpoint's early days its most active members were women who were willing to turn their hand to any job that needed doing. Joan Marshall, who joined the Viewpoint staff in 1979, received the impression that 'Miss Cunningham got houses and let others do the running'. 'The running' meant everything from managing waiting lists to checking electrical fitments. When one journalist visited the fourth Viewpoint property, Deborah House, prior to its opening in 1949, she discovered 'a prominent member of the Electrical Association for Women' (with husband in tow) 'busily engaged in fitting up light bulbs and plugs'.[37] 'The members of the voluntary committee do much of the preparatory work themselves – scrubbing, cleaning, and polishing', confirmed the Society's Secretary, Miss Ellis. 'I do not know of any men's organisation which could have done so much so cheaply.'

A letter written by a recently installed caretaker at Bridget House to an English women's magazine of the day supports Miss Ellis's observation. She praised the 'small group of retired spinsters' for their work. The magazine editor responded in kind:

> *All praise to the women who have tackled a problem so sensibly, economically and humanly* [sic]*. They would be*

Scots, of course – what a genius for organization that great little nation has.

But even genius has its hurdles to overcome and Viewpoint had its fair share of them during this period of expansion. Two letters to the *Scotsman* in August 1951 indicate that public perception was one of them. An exchange had already been printed between Miss Merrylees of the National Federation of Housing Societies and a local Edinburgh councillor, Mrs Muir. Referring to Housing Societies that served only one section of society, Mrs Muir had had the temerity to suggest that they were operating 'with selfish ends.' This remark drew the wrath of George Barr, Secretary to the Scottish regional branch of the NFHS, and of Miss Cunningham herself.

Government policy, explained George Barr, dictated that Housing Societies confine their efforts to specified special categories: the housing and care of older people (for example in Edinburgh, Glasgow and Perth – and more recently Hawick and Jedburgh), and housing for industrial workers (Grangemouth, Paisley), disabled ex-servicemen (Renfrew, Perth) and single women (Edinburgh).

In the total of 423 affiliated societies in the Federation, over 160 are working for the housing and care of old people, by far the majority of which are in the retirement pension income group.[38]

Councillor Muir had implied that Housing Societies had not been working in close cooperation with Local

Authorities. Mr Barr responded: 'Even a superficial knowledge of housing legislation shows that ... no housing society can build anywhere without the approval of the statutory bodies concerned and the nomination of tenants has to be agreed in every case with those bodies'. As Miss Merrylees herself had indicated during the Edinburgh housing conference four years earlier, Housing Societies were under no illusion about the importance of keeping in with Local Authorities.

Miss Cunningham, in *her* letter, suggested what subsequent historians have confirmed, that the situation in Scotland was harder than in England, and she indicated that the problem of inaccurate perception went far beyond the remarks of one Edinburgh councillor:

> *While welcoming the enthusiasm and optimism of the founders of the housing crusade, those of us who have been long in touch with the NFHS feel that the education of the public in the housing society movement is incomplete without full knowledge of what has to be faced, as well as what has already been achieved.*[39]

She goes on to dismiss the notion that specialised Housing Societies are working for selfish ends, 'seeing that every effort to reduce the housing problem in some section aids in diminishing the whole'.

A more immediate concern for Viewpoint, however, was a decision by Edinburgh's Property Valuation Committee to increase substantially the rents payable by Viewpoint on its properties. For example, 5 Northumberland Street (Bridget House) had previously been assessed at £90. Now it had been reassessed at £323.

The Valuation Committee took the view that each rented room should be categorised as a separate residence, rather than assessing the whole property as a single unit. It was a potential problem to which the Viewpoint Committee had been alerted some time previously following a Court of Appeal decision in England. In June 1948, the Court had ruled on a case in Birmingham, concluding that tenants of separate flats who shared the use of a kitchen within a house were not protected by the Rent Restrictions Act. By the autumn of 1949, Mr George Cheyne was having to argue the same matter on Viewpoint's behalf before Edinburgh's Valuation Committee.

A newspaper report describes the case, which had been heard the previous day.[40] Mr Cheyne explained that the Viewpoint properties had been purchased by appealing for loan stock investors. When £1000 had been promised, a house was bought. Half of the money went towards the purchase and the other half was used for redecoration and necessary alterations. No structural alterations were made. Crucially, he says that the Society purchased properties for its own members. Therefore, he argued, 'the ordinary principle of landlord and tenant did not apply. These houses should be treated as owner-occupied and assessed as units, and each room should not be assessed separately'. George Cheyne also attempted to prick the public conscience by emphasising the social good that Viewpoint was contributing to the city (the same argument used by Miss Cunningham in her letter to the *Scotsman*). The Society, Mr Cheyne contended, was providing a necessary service to a sector of society that Edinburgh Local Authority (unlike the Glasgow Corporation) was not yet serving. In other words, everyone benefited from the work that Viewpoint had undertaken.

The court's decision was only a partial victory for Viewpoint. The assessor amended the rents but still argued that the presence of individual tenants meant that he could not treat the houses each as *unum quid*. Instead, he treated them as if they were blocks of serviced flats. The Bridget House assessment was therefore reduced from £323 to £280 and the assessments of Anne and Charlotte Houses were reduced by a similar percentage. Miss Cunningham reported to Viewpoint's Fourth Annual General Meeting the following February that only a change of law by Parliament would allow the assessor to take an alternative approach.

Columnist Alison Settle, in her 'Woman's Viewpoint' column[41], was unimpressed. Under the heading 'Tax Injustices', she highlighted the Viewpoint case and argued that had Viewpoint run its properties as boarding houses an assessment of £250 would have been reduced to just £53. 'This is something of which other housing societies need to be aware,' she warned.

The 'vexed question' of assessments would be of continuing concern for some years and Viewpoint would even consider going to court over the issue.[42] To the dismay of the Committee, however, one resident of Anne House took matters into her own hands. It was brought to the Committee's attention that Miss Pitbladdo had instructed the Homeless Association to appeal to the Rent Tribunal for a reduction of rent. This, the Committee considered, 'was to have acted to the "detriment of the Society".[43] It was also the straw that broke the camel's back, for Miss Pitbladdo's action came on top of a succession of complaints made by her and a consequent mood of growing unrest in Anne House. Despite its not unsympathetic negotiations with Miss Pitbladdo, in the end the Committee felt compelled to force her hand. It brought forward a motion to expel Miss Pitbladdo from the Society – and therefore from her tenancy. It was thought that the prospect of such a motion might be enough to persuade her to resign of her own accord, which it did.

In the same year of the row over assessments, Viewpoint opened its third and fourth houses: Deborah House at 2 Mansionhouse Road in Edinburgh's Grange area (a substantial detached property bought for under £3,000), and Eleanor House at 32 Craigmillar Park. The long waiting list for places is evidence of continuing enthusiasm for the developments. The Society had about 280 members by the time Eleanor House was opened, encouraged no doubt by what were still considered low rents for attractive properties. The rents for this latest property ranged from eight shillings to 35, which the Committee intended to reduce once loans for the purchase had been paid off.

In Deborah House, 'one large airy room with three bay windows on the second floor will be in the 25s group,' reported the *Evening News* – adding, however, that the room with the best view was in the attic space. Miss Cockburn told the reporter that hundreds of applications for membership had even been received from married couples, many of them citing cases of exorbitant prices being asked for rooms.

*Indeed, [Miss Cockburn] states, some couples would pay
almost anything to have a room of their own and she is
only sorry that, with the absolute restrictions on private
building, the Society can do nothing to expand their
membership in an effort to ease the situation.*[44]

This would be a continuing problem for Viewpoint.
Former warden, Marjorie Sinclair, recalls that in the late
seventies, people would get on the waiting list through
word of mouth. Because Edinburgh is a small city, she
says, 'people would talk.' Hopeful individuals would come
to her at the Gillespie Crescent property and say, 'I hear
someone has died – can I see the flat?'

Such was the demand in the early days that periodically the waiting list had to be closed. When it was
reopened in April 1950 in time to receive applications for
Eleanor House, the membership nearly doubled in just
four weeks and the Committee felt obliged to close the
list once more, 'realising it would be unjustifiable to
continue increasing the number of members beyond
that which they could reasonably hope to accommodate.'[45] It was a situation mirrored throughout the
country, as Alison Settle explained in her 'Woman's
Viewpoint' column, noting that 'another body with flatlet
houses for professional women is also withholding statements because they receive at least a hundred applications for every rumoured vacancy.'[46]

Alison Settle's article draws special attention to the
Federation of Soroptimist Clubs. Founded in California in
1921, this was an international organisation that strove to
achieve 'the best for women' in every sphere of their lives.
Their motto was: 'Working for the world we want.' By the

early 1950s, 59 of the 177 Soroptimist Clubs in Britain had set up Housing Associations intended to provide accommodation for women but they, like other housing organisations, had had to re-think their ambitions. Though the Association's branch in Halifax owned a block of 40 new flatlets, in the main the Soroptimists had had to shift from the post-war dream of building new properties to converting older ones. The FSC published a book, *Soroptimist Housing*, which dealt with comparative conversion and building costs and addressed questions of management, mortgages and loans. But demand, the report continues, was outstripping supply:

> *What they have achieved, though creditable, is so small compared to the total demand that, says the Federation, they have been chary of giving details or even locations of existing homes, thinking it cruel to raise false hopes.*[47]

Reporting to the Viewpoint AGM in February 1951, Miss Ellis was of the view that 'the faraway future seemed rosy, and in thirty years the Society should own most of its houses, and be quite a rich concern. The immediate future, however, was not clear.'[48]

None of these difficulties prevented Viewpoint from developing new ideas. A model self-contained flatlet went on display at around this time in a home design exhibition hosted by the National Gallery in London. It drew 'many comments of approval from women visitors,' according to Louise Morgan in an article headed 'Houseful of Homes'. She went on to say that 'the pooled experience of the [Soroptimist] clubs has shown that the bed-sitting room flatlet with bath can be set at an economic rent, and that conversion of old houses provides better accommodation than building new blocks of flats.'

The Viewpoint Committee was already considering its own such provision of self-contained accommodation, but putting their plans into practice would take time. In the meantime, though, the living arrangements for Eleanor House indicate that the original model of communal living was requiring a re-think. Asked about the ease of maintaining a 'happy home' in a community living setting, Miss Cockburn put up a positive front, saying that the only objection she recalled being raised had to do with the keeping of a cat in one residence. In reality, the high hopes for good community relations that had accompanied the opening of Anne House had foundered in the kitchen. In a piece headed with dry understatement 'Women in the kitchen don't always agree', the *Evening News* reported:

> *The truth of the belief that women find it difficult amicably to share a kitchen is one of the lessons learned by the housing manager of the Viewpoint Housing Society Ltd in the course of running their first four houses for single women in Edinburgh.*[49]

In a colourful description that sounds more like an episode of TV's *Big Brother* than the early days of an innovative housing organisation, Miss Ingham recalled vividly the situation that developed at Anne House:

> *We had great faith in the reasonableness of human beings but this faith was nearly shattered. It should have been*

*possible to arrange a rota for the use of the kitchen, but
what really operated was the law of the jungle. Pans and
kettles were snatched off stoves, washing pulled off the
pulleys [and] lawyers' letters began to fly back and forth
as tenants fell out with each other. The lonely haunted the
kitchen in search of company, deputations would descend
upon the poor Secretary in the office accusing each other
of mild, ridiculous, domestic demeanours. We felt as if the
war had finished up in our house.*[50]

Even allowing for a touch of dramatic licence in the
telling, Anne House was not the domestic Eden that the
Committee had hoped for. There needed to be a re-
assessment of the facilities provided for tenants. Miss
Ingham speaks of kitchens with three cookers and three
sinks ('although it must have been a strain for tenants, it
was an improvement') but it seems that it wasn't until
house number five that such improvements actually took
effect. 'When [Eleanor House] opens in a week or two,'
said the 'Eve's Circle' article, 'the fruit of this experience
will be incorporated, and no more than two residents
will have to share the same gas stove or washing-up facilities.'

Nevertheless, it was inevitable that issues relating to
community life would continue to arise. The Committee
could be extremely firm in such matters, as the case of
Miss Pitbladdo suggests. Equally, it is clear that the
women went out of their way to reach charitable
compromises where possible, even if this meant allowing
a matter to drag on for some time. The difficulties
encountered by the residents of Charlotte House with
one of their number resulted in discussions with lawyers

and talk of the Court of Session. In the end, however, the matter was discussed at length with the residents themselves and, there being no unanimity about how to address the situation, the resident in question was put on probation. As the Society's solicitor, Mr Cheyne, said, here was a woman 70 years of age: 'the Court might consider the hardship for her greater were she evicted from Charlotte House than the hardship to the Society were she allowed to remain.'[51]

On other occasions, attempts to offer a creative solution proved less welcome. An invitation to the residents of Deborah House to keep the water in the lavatory pans clean and to use the available brushes met with high indignation from one resident who said that placing such a notice in bathrooms 'led to suspicion and bad feeling among the tenants.' The Committee duly apologised – while underlining its responsibility for the cleanliness of residences.[52]

In fact, the lavatory pan incident had arisen from the Committee's attempts to encourage the Deborah House caretaker to raise the House's overall standards of clean-liness. As with all the early Viewpoint properties, accom-modation was provided for a caretaker. But since little or no other payment was made for this work, other than perhaps a Spring Cleaning bonus or an end of year gratuity, the Committee had few options at their disposal if problems needed resolving.

Such niggles as had to be dealt with, however, should be placed within the context of the Committee's care for its unpaid members of staff. A Minute dated October 14, 1952 notes the Committee's regret that 'it could not yet see its way to pay the caretakers for their services in addition to the present exchange of room, light and heat for service, but agreed that where elderly single women were engaged a cleaner should be sent once a month for heavy work. In December the following year the Committee discussed two caretakers who had both given three to four years of service but who, it was realised, might not be able to continue working for very much longer. It was agreed that they be made members of the Society, thus making it possible to offer them a room, 'and if the rent was going to prove a difficulty, [the secretary] would investigate what help could be given by the Public Assistance Board'.[53]

Deborah House had added eleven more rooms to Viewpoint's list, as well as accommodation for a caretaker. With further space for ten women, Eleanor House brought the total number of women now housed by Viewpoint to 50, with older members of the Society generally getting priority. The policy 'has always been to offer rooms to their members on the basis of greatest need,' reports the *Evening News*, 'with length of membership and financial circumstances as influential factors'. However, Viewpoint was also beginning to feel the pull of rising expectations. The same report notes the increasing difficulty of letting some of Viewpoint's rooms. The basement rooms, with their lack of view and prospect of footsteps treading the pavements above them, were understandably less popular, but so too were the larger, and therefore more expensive, rooms.

'Room G' in Fiona House (opened in November 1950) was a case in point. Formerly this room had been the ground floor drawing room of the house, but the Committee found it being 'taken definitely on several occasions and then renounced'.[54] It was always considered too big or too expensive, yet the Committee considered it worth a higher rent than the room immediately above it.

Regarding such rooms, Miss Ingham offers a slightly ambivalent response that hints at the fact that the Viewpoint Committee was considering alternative housing solutions. She was well aware 'that 30s to 35s is a lot to ask for an unfurnished room ... but there are still women, accustomed to living in their own house, who prefer a room in a good property where they can have their own furniture to living in "digs"'. Marjory Sinclair, speaking of her experience over three decades later, reinforces that point even more strongly. By bringing their own furniture, tenants made their rooms 'home' – 'and this is what prolonged their lives.'

There would always be a tricky balance to maintain between providing the basic facilities that residents required – the need to offer the degree of privacy and independence that they desired – and the growing imperative to acquire properties in areas that were desirable to the 'business and professional' women Viewpoint sought to support. There was an attraction in being able to live in or near an area close to one's friends, to familiar haunts or one's church. Increasingly, though, Viewpoint was also dealing with women who were prepared to pay more to achieve the kind of balance that they wanted. This certainly seems to have been one factor in Miss Cunningham's decision at this point to form a second, quite separate, Housing Society – the Four Freedoms Housing Society Ltd.

Chapter 6

Four Freedoms

Very little documentation relating to Four Freedoms has survived. The Viewpoint archives hold one book of loan stock certificates and a news cutting from 'Eve's Circle' dated May 25, 1951. Most of what we can easily discern about the new Society is drawn from Viewpoint Minutes and these reflect an attitude towards Miss Cunningham's new venture that can only be described as ambivalent. This impression may be due simply to a quite proper decision not to record comments about another Society except where matters pertained quite particularly to Viewpoint itself. Perhaps, also, there was some concern about competition from another Society, and even unease, at this stage in Viewpoint's development, that Miss Cunningham had opted to go it alone. There is no firm evidence to support this conjecture, but later Minute entries on the subject convey a noticeably cool tone, albeit a business-like one.

Precisely why Miss Cunningham took the step she did, we do not know – though presumably she felt there was room for more than one Housing Society in Edinburgh for older, single women. The first we – and members of the Committee – hear about her plan is in a Viewpoint Minute dated December 2, 1950. Miss Cunningham, it reads, thinks that the Committee should know that she is trying to form another Society to which some Viewpoint members might like to transfer. Her reason for making that suggestion must be based on the growing awareness that some women have the means to pay more for housing accommodation but are, as the Minute reports it, 'too old to take out a bond with a building society':

> With guarantees, this [could] be done on their behalf by the Society, with the Co-operative Permanent Building Society, and the cost of alterations [to the new properties] [could] be shared among the tenants and the new Society.

Having received this news, the Committee is then asked by Miss Cunningham to consider producing joint publicity for the two Societies. She appears to be moving fast – faster than most of the Committee would like. The Committee defer a decision until after the next AGM, 'as mention of the subject could probably be made during the discussion it was proposed to hold'. In the event, there is no record of direct reference to Four Freedoms at the next AGM (1951) and the next time there is any discussion about joint publicity – within an article that Miss Cunningham proposes to write for the Housing Federation Bulletin – it is decided to omit any mention of Four Freedoms for fear that readers would assume a connection between the two Societies.[55] What *is* discussed at the AGM the following February is the question of how much Viewpoint should or can expand its housing stock. Miss Cunningham reports that after the Membership List had been reopened in April 1950, following one of its periods of closure, the membership had nearly doubled in four weeks – leading to another closure of the list, it being 'unjustifiable to continue increasing the number of members beyond that which [the Society] could reasonably hope to accommodate.'[56] Despite this evidence of Viewpoint's popularity, however, in the discussion that follows, the Secretary, Miss Ellis, recommends surveying the existing members in order to ascertain 'exactly how many more houses would really be needed, as [the Society] could not go on forever buying them. When she asked members who wished for rooms to hold up their hands, some 24 members responded.'[57]

Is Miss Cunningham concerned that Viewpoint is not moving forward with enough ambition? Does she sense that her original vision has now been taken out of her hands? Whatever agreements or disagreements there might have been about Viewpoint's relationship with Four Freedoms, by May 1951 'Eve's Circle' was reporting that the new Society had been established in March of that year.[58] It is reported that initial membership was limited to one hundred and that over fifty had already enrolled. In fact, the certificate book seems to show nothing like that number. However, the original Viewpoint Register of Members indicates that, at some point, many members did indeed transfer a majority of their shares to loan stock and it is possible, though by no means certain, that some of these transfers had to do with the formation of Four Freedoms.

The use of loan stock had been referred to by George Cheyne during his appeal to the Edinburgh Valuation Committee. It was a method of self-financing that Viewpoint would employ at various times throughout its history. Notably, it would take on a crucial role during the 1970s when loan stock schemes enabled Viewpoint to establish two independent housing projects, Croft-an-Righ and Kilravock. It seems that Four Freedoms represents one occasion prior to that period when the principle was also put into action in order to bankroll a complete project. In 1951, however, the scheme operated with two significant differences.

Loan stock was a way of funding a building to be subsequently let rather than sold for owner occupation. The cost of purchasing a property, probably using a Building Society loan, was met by raising loans that in effect guaranteed an ability to pay the Building Society back. In the 1970s, the opportunity to purchase stock would be confined to prospective tenants, but in the case of Four Freedoms, it could be purchased both by tenants and also by interested investors. Stock was purchased on the understanding that it would be paid back either to the investor or her estate at a fixed interest rate of three per cent – another difference from later schemes, which paid no interest.

Four Freedoms, of which Miss Cunningham was once again Chair, used the increased purchasing power granted by loan stock in combination with a cooperative approach. The name of the Society, reports 'Eve's Circle', was 'partly self-explanatory'. It refers to the speech made by President Roosevelt to the American Congress in 1941, at the point when America was planning to enter the Second World War. He had used the address to describe the kinds of freedom that Americans were prepared to fight for – and which echoed Miss Cunningham's own deep-felt values: the freedom of speech, the freedom of worship, the freedom from want, and the freedom from fear.

The name also reflected the four plans which the organisers of the new Society hoped to operate when conditions permitted. First, it was proposed that groups of between eight and ten members, each requiring one good room with facilities, should lend the Society £100 each, to be repaid at the close of their tenancy, in order to deliver the Society enough funds to acquire and adapt a suitable house. In the first instance, Four Freedoms intended to convert two such properties. Each tenant would be responsible for her own decoration and furnishing, and rents would be set at £1 or 25 shillings a week – presumably lower than they would have been without payment of loan stock in the first place. The rents would cover general cleaning but no 'personal services.'

Second, if there were those who desired a flat of two or three rooms then loan stock to the value of £250 – £350 per person would be purchased from a group of three or four women and a property then purchased on the same basis. To date, Viewpoint had never attempted anything so ambitious as to offer more than one room per person – and the way things turned out for Four Freedoms confirms the wisdom of the Committee's discretion. Thirdly, it was hoped that, when funds built up, a further house could be purchased and rooms let to individual tenants 'who might not have capital to join either of the other two plans' – in other words, on the same basis as all Viewpoint's early 'alphabet houses.' And the fourth plan was to 'provide accommodation for younger business and professional women on a short-term basis.'

It is not clear to what extent these four plans were all followed through or, indeed, which properties Four

Freedoms purchased as a result of the loan stock scheme. What is interesting is that, while the majority of the certificates record individual purchase of between £100 and £250 worth of loan stock, occasionally much smaller amounts were purchased. This indicates either that there was more flexibility within the system than the newspaper reports suggest, or that, as in the case of Viewpoint, there were those willing to lend or invest money in what they considered to be a good cause.

Nothing more is heard about Four Freedoms until February 1960, fewer than nine years after its inception, when the Viewpoint Committee receives a letter from Miss Cunningham asking Viewpoint to consider taking over Four Freedoms.[59] Miss Cunningham had remained as chairman of Viewpoint until spring 1958, at which point she decided not to stand for re-election at the forthcoming AGM. She chairs her last Committee meeting on April 11th and eleven days later Miss C M Brown (later 'Rankine Brown') is elected as her successor.[60] Miss Cunningham's last official duty for Viewpoint was to preside over the AGM on the 15th.

Clearly the question of taking over Four Freedoms is a matter for the lawyers in the first instance. However, 'both Miss Cockburn and Miss Moyse felt that the dissolving of Four Freedoms would be the best solution. If the houses were taken over by Viewpoint their occupants should not become members of Viewpoint.' This seemingly hard-line stance was to be softened by further negotiations.

At the beginning of April 1960, it was reported that the Four Freedoms Society Committee had passed a resolution indicating that it wished to form a merger with Viewpoint, though this decision needed to be put to a General Meeting of Four Freedoms. In the meantime, Viewpoint had commissioned two surveys of the Four Freedoms properties, neither of which produced positive results.[61] The valuer had estimated a market value for the properties of £9,200, though Bonds on the properties amounted to £9,000 and loan stock amounted to just £3,000.

> *The Committee made it quite clear that the only reason they were prepared to consider the matter at all was because of possible repercussions should a Housing Society in Edinburgh fail to meet its obligations and because it should not be forgotten that Miss J M M Cunningham, the founder of Four Freedoms had also been the initiator of the Viewpoint Housing Society Ltd.*[62]

The Committee's instinct was that Four Freedoms should go into liquidation and Viewpoint take over responsibility for properties, loan stock and existing tenants. However, Viewpoint's legal adviser, Mr Cheyne, advised against going down this route as it would necessitate selling the properties on the open market to meet the Bond holders' claims, leaving nothing for loan stock holders. With some reluctance, therefore, the Committee voted to proceed with negotiations for a take-over. Five members abstained from the vote and only four voted for it.

In April, the Viewpoint Committee clarified its terms. Concerned about the state of the Four Freedoms properties it was agreed that, in the event of a merger, they should be sold as soon as possible 'and that a condition of the take over of Four Freedoms should be that its members relinquish their membership shares.[63] It was also confirmed that 'only loan stock holders and present tenants should become members of the Viewpoint Housing Society'. For whatever reason – reluctance or simply the slow turning of Committee of affairs, Four Freedoms was slow to respond to this conditional offer – nothing had been heard from them by November 19th. But records indicate that in 1961, the Four Freedoms Society was finally incorporated into Viewpoint by 'transfer of engagements'.

The short history of Four Freedoms is a reminder that the success of a venture such as this was not a foregone conclusion. The Viewpoint Committee's concerns about the property Four Freedoms owned hints that some of Viewpoint's own success was derived from an ability to make astute property acquisitions that were attractive to its core clientele. Four Freedoms also appears to have stretched itself beyond its means, another flaw that Viewpoint avoided. However, though the Four Freedoms episode was evidently a source of some discomfort for the Viewpoint Committee, it perhaps had the effect of re-galvanising Viewpoint's own ambitions. By the time the negotiations with Four Freedoms had been concluded, Viewpoint had taken out new mortgages on its very first properties, Anne House and Bridget House, in order to fund improvements to them. In addition, Viewpoint had begun instigating plans that went well beyond the basic formula of bed-sits established with Anne House. The Committee wanted more for Edinburgh's single women, and more varied and flexible funding methods were now making this possible.

The person to drive these ambitions forward was Miss Ann Evelyn Ingham. A founding member of Viewpoint, in 1952 she took over the role of Secretary and would become the dominant personality of the organisation for the next four decades.

Chapter 7
Miss Ingham

On November 1, 1982, Miss Ingham wrote to Etta Whyte, manager of Viewpoint's budget shop in the Tanfield area of Edinburgh. Etta's team had recently hosted a Coffee Morning in aid of the Target £1 Million Fund, launched in 1980 to raise money for a new facility for the frail elderly. Etta's note of accounts for the year 1982–83 show that the event raised £1,070 in addition to the shop's own income for the year of £8,992. Thirty years after being appointed Secretary of Viewpoint, Miss Ingham's enthusiastic response still conveyed an irrepressible commitment to the organisation as well as her characteristic attention to the personal contributions of others.

> *There has never been anyone quite like the "Budget Shop Gang" ... How many pounds of marmalade go to make up £100? I know it represents a lot of steamy kitchens and a lot of hardwork* [sic]. *Then I was interested to see that Miss Conner is still dressing dolls. In fact all of the helpers deserve a special vote of thanks for hardwork beyond the call of duty ...*

Of the Target Fund itself, she writes:

> *I wonder if I told you that I had looked up Webster's* Dictionary *for a definition and I found Target: a Targe*

*or buckler, a shield. I think it is lovely to feel that we are
working to provide a shield or buckler for our older friends
in time of need. I think as time goes on we may learn to
call our type of Home "Targe Homes". It has a good
Scottish ring about it.*

In January 1952, Miss Ellis, Viewpoint's first Secretary-
Manager, had let it be known that she wished to step
down from that position and so the Committee set about
finding a successor. Initially, it looked outside its own
ranks, with both Miss Ellis and Miss Cunningham
putting forward names for consideration. In particular,
the Committee considered Miss MacWillan Wilson,
formerly a school secretary, with knowledge of book
keeping and, significantly, experience of letting out her
own house to business and professional women on much
the same model as Viewpoint. Moreover, she was willing
to take on the job for the same honorarium as Miss Ellis.

The Minutes record that it was at this point, the
Committee having already taken the step of meeting
Miss Wilson, that Miss Moyse asked 'whether there was
no one on the Committee who would take on the post;
their experience from the beginning would be so
valuable.'[64] She named specifically Mrs Falconer and Miss
Ingham, a founder member of Viewpoint. Because Mrs
Falconer was fully committed to the Electrical
Association of Women, it was left to Miss Ingham to
ponder the idea. One week later, she asked to be
considered.

On the face of it, Miss Ingham's qualifications fall a
little short against Miss Wilson's. Born in 1913, she had
been trained as an interior decorator and ran an arts and

crafts shop on Edinburgh's Rose Street. During the war, she had worked for the Civil Service as a 'Regional Arts Exhibitionist for Scotland.' No doubt, the Committee was aware of her other qualities, however, and perhaps of her possible contacts. Her father was closely involved with the Edinburgh Council and one might imagine that political savvy and a commitment to public service had been passed on as family traits. Unfettered by today's expectations of job selection criteria and professional references, it doesn't appear to have taken the Committee much time to offer Miss Ingham the job and the Minutes of February 18 record her acceptance. She undertook the work in a part-time capacity, having offered the Committee two days per week. Part-time jobs, however, rarely remain that way for long, as Miss Ingham must have well known.

Like Miss Cunningham, there was a religious dimension to Miss Ingham's commitment to Viewpoint. Writing to Marjory Sinclair in 1986, she mused: 'If only we could always see the real man; that would be a better place.' She refers to an unspecified 'new challenge' and suggests that it is 'really an opportunity to move "above the salt"':

> Forgive me, – I am not preaching, I am just looking for an answer for myself and inflicting it on you. But it is painfully obvious that material law and persons are not going to solve the world's problems. Therefore we have to look for another answers [sic].

It was an ethos that wardens like Marjory Sinclair shared. It was always about seeing the person, not the problem, explains Marjory Sinclair. 'Always when people were being particularly difficult, which old people can be, you had to look for the root cause of the problem.' If a tenant came complaining about a faulty tap, for example, the question to ask was whether it was the tap that was at fault or whether the individual was simply lonely because her family hadn't contacted her in a while. Miss Ingham was ever the Secretary of Underlying Causes, and over the years staff members like Marjory responded warmly to that approach.

She was not, however, a born administrator. She was no good at organising, recalls Jack Fleming, Viewpoint Chairman from 1985 until 1991. 'She inspired but she wasn't organised – so it was up to others to help keep the show on the road.' People like Joan Stephenson, who had trained under the auspices of the Society of Women Housing Managers and who arrived at Viewpoint with her Royal Institute of Chartered Surveyors qualification and experience of housing work in Edinburgh, Chelsea, Mauritius and Cumbernauld. On her first day in the Northumberland Street office in 1975, she asked to see the agreements for Viewpoint's two hundred tenants. 'I knew it!' exclaimed Miss Ingham. 'I knew you'd want paper. They do [have agreements] but I haven't done them all yet.' Joan was eventually handed some agreements in a box file, only to discover that each and every one was dated 1971. 'Miss Ingham didn't think that paperwork was worth anything,' Joan Marshall agrees. 'She trusted the whole world and expected them to trust her.' She believed that people would do what she said. 'If she told them not to hang their washing out on a Saturday, they wouldn't.'

Miss Ingham's antipathy towards red tape no doubt brought successive Chairmen out in a cold sweat, several of them having previously worked within the rigorously methodical structures of the Civil Service. Former members of staff, however, mostly remember her for other gifts, especially as a communicator and encourager. Typically, Joan Marshall recalls taking part in a hundred-hole golf tournament to raise funds for Viewpoint. This marathon required a 6am start but Miss Ingham was there to see the golfers off and there at the end to welcome them in with bouquets (as was Jack Fleming, at that time Chairman of Viewpoint's fund raising arm, Viewpoint Benevolent). 'She would come past your desk,' says Joan,' put a sweet on it and say "Good morning". She pulled our strings in the nicest way – you just found yourself volunteering.' Marjory Sinclair goes further than that. Her view is that all the women who worked for Viewpoint 'needed to be needed'.

> *This is why they worked for Viewpoint – and this is why Viewpoint got very high class-staff. Miss Ingham used their skills, and you worked doubly hard of course.*

Moreover, for all that Miss Ingham was a reluctant administrator, she was quick to grasp opportunities when they arose and kept a close eye on legislative changes in the social housing arena. In the mid-1950s, housing policy was changing a good deal, opportunities were there for the taking and Miss Ingham would ensure that Viewpoint took full advantage of them.

Towards the end of 1950, Fiona House had been opened, offering rooms for twelve more tenants (including the stubbornly un-lettable former drawing room, 'Room G'). This was followed by Gillian House, which had been found with some difficulty. Susan Maclennan notes that at around this time a house-hunting sub-committee was established, but it appears that Miss Cunningham was still the Society's nominated 'House Hunter'. On January 30, 1951, she proposed a number of steps to the Committee, including building a flat on top of Anne House and the consideration of 14 Claremont Park, both proposals rejected by the Committee. (It is notable that, despite being Viewpoint's founder, Miss Cunningham doesn't dominate its development. Indeed, on more than one occasion the Minutes record that her ideas failed to meet with Committee approval.[65]) The Committee did agree to look at another property in Claremont Park and one on Newhaven Road but the former proved too expensive and the latter unavailable. In the end it was the house at number 48 Morningside Park that took the name of 'Gillian', opening in September that year.

A request from Gillian House tenants a few months later provides one example of the Committee's ideas about the running of its houses, departing from standard procedure only with reluctance. The tenants had asked to be able to use gas rings in their rooms for cooking. The Committee decided that this would be allowable, 'but that the Manager should discourage it'.[66]

With the purchase of Viewpoint's eighth house, however, the gas ring question was no longer an issue. For the first time, announced Miss Cunningham, it had been possible 'to eliminate entirely the shared kitchenette'.[67] More significant still, Hester House (15 Northumberland

Street) represented a first step towards making greater use of public funding for Viewpoint projects, encouraged by Miss Ingham's desire to approach the Edinburgh Corporation for loan and improvement grants. The new property was acquired through a building society loan of £3,250. In addition, arrangements for an improvement loan were made through the Edinburgh Corporation. A firm of civil engineers, Carfrae and Morrison, were employed to do the work on the understanding that they would forego their fee should the application for improvements fail.

Hester House would become home not only to eleven more tenants but also to the Viewpoint office. It had moved once already, from its original location at 11 Rutland Street to 12 Drummond Place (Fiona House) but the Northumberland Street location offered slightly more space, was a little nearer the tramcar route and the condition of the basement would present a better impression of the Society to visitors and enquirers. None of these matters were insignificant as the Viewpoint office had always been a place of comings and goings. The Society had prided itself on having office opening hours that enabled professional women to make enquiries after work. Rent payments were made in person to the office, either by individual tenants or through the caretakers – 'thus saving the salary of a rent collector', observed Miss Ellis. At the desk, too, volunteers were used for receiving payments. Miss Stuart, who moved into Charlotte House on Newhaven Road as a young woman (this was not simply an organisation for the elderly) and brought with her accounting skills, was one of a rota of tenants who acted as rent collectors in the office. Joan Stephenson recalls sub-contractors presenting their bills at the office counter after rents had been brought in. They were paid out of the cash that had now accumulated in the drawer.

Two other, and more far-reaching, developments took place in the early 1950s, partly in response to changing housing legislation. The first was the decision to seek charitable status. To this point, Viewpoint had been registered with the Registrar of Friendly Societies as a non-profit organisation but that did not exempt the Society from having to make substantial payments of Income Tax. The Committee reported to the 1953 AGM that, as a result, it was experiencing some concern about the Society's future.

> *It now appeared that as the mortgages on the houses were decreased with the passing years, a greater proportion of the income drawn from rents would be liable to tax, although this money was already ear-marked for the repayment of loan stock.*[68]

For this reason, the Committee proposed the change of status, which (though it took a while for the benefits to be felt) brought the Society into line with other non-profit organisations.

The second significant development was Viewpoint's campaign to secure government funding for the Society's and – in the view of Norman Dunhill – Scotland's first purpose-built flats for single women. Miss Ingham's initial thought had been to form a new Society to take this work and Viewpoint's other projects forward. On October 25, 1951, before the purchase of Hester House, she argued that the existing structure and staffing could not support further developments. Surprisingly, one of the reasons she gives is that the office couldn't cope with any more rents being paid on a Thursday. She proposed 'leaving the old [Society] to consolidate its position and begin paying its debts'[69] and to use the new financing opportunities (utilised for Hester House) as the spur for establishing a second organisation. No discussion is reported and the notion of 'The New Viewpoint Society Ltd' was shelved. Nevertheless, the idea of a fresh start had been planted, and by the time of the AGM the following February, it had been agreed that the first seven houses should be regarded as a single 'unit' on which to base a budget for a further seven houses.

Viewpoint records exude a renewed sense of purpose at this time. Its mood mirrored the times. The Conservatives, led by Winston Churchill and subsequently Anthony Eden, were re-elected into government under the slogan 'Turn Hopes into Homes'. The Minister for Housing, Harold Macmillan, had set about building 300,000 new council houses per year. The 1949 Housing Act allowed for greater assistance than previously for reconditioning work, at the discretion of Local Authorities, and it seems that Viewpoint's track record was standing it in good stead. In 1954, the Government would relax restrictions on improvement grants still further. Meanwhile, the hunt was on (no longer just by Miss Cunningham) for suitable properties (number 16 Chalmers Crescent was one result), and the energetic involvement of Miss Ingham was increasingly evident. Above all, plans for new 'flatlets' seem to have put a spring in the Committee's corporate step.

The plans for the flats were revealed to the 'Eve's

Circle' columnist who reported that the blocks of flats were to be three storeys high and to feature 'paladin bins' for the disposal of rubbish down a chute. This ventilated chute led to a sealed-off bin that was accessed from outside. Each flat would have its own small bathroom, kitchen, living room and bedroom and rent would be no higher than for a similar Corporation flat. Miss Ingham was quoted as saying that the Corporation 'are now realising that such organisations [as Viewpoint] are an asset and are to be encouraged'. At any rate, the report concludes, 'the work of Viewpoint Society is bound to relieve the housing authorities of part of their worries concerning single women'.[70]

The layout of the flats, not dissimilar to the model apartments exhibited at the National Gallery, were a substantial step up from the bed-sits of the first 'alphabet houses', but it had taken some determination to bring Edinburgh Council on board. Miss Cunningham's view was that, while government legislation had long been favourable to housing societies, it had proved until now difficult to persuade the Local Authority of the fact. It had 'been necessary to show them how to overcome some of the difficulties'.[71] That Viewpoint was successful in its bid to build new properties owed a good deal to Miss Ingham's astute reading of the new housing legislation. For all that she was averse to red tape, she kept a copy of the Act by her bedside and she later recalled the eureka moment that made progress seem possible.

No one in Scotland knew much about Housing Associations, and the first attempts to secure a grant went astray because even the [Scottish Office] officials could

> not direct us in how to use the provisionsof the Housing
> Acts ... It was at this time that we discovered that housing
> finance only provided 80% of the cost, the remaining 20%
> had to be raised by the association. As private lenders
> would only lend for a few years at a time this was
> untenable. No Association could possibly build if all its
> efforts were to be continually channelled into searching
> for replacements for the 20%.
>
> Then one night, or early morning – 2 a.m. to be exact,
> the Secretary wakened up, convinced that there was a
> solution, and picking up the Housing Act – bedside
> reading – she opened it to a section which said, a Local
> Authority could invest in an approved project. So back to
> the City Chambers, where the Burgh Treasurer agreed that
> this was indeed an approved project, and Viewpoint was
> doing something that the Local Authority was not able to
> do at that time, notably helping single people.[72]

In the autumn of 1953, Miss Ingham reported on a positive
meeting held with the City Chamberlain, Ames Imrie.
Viewpoint representatives were told that the legislation
did exist to help them but that it now depended on how
the Society approached the relevant committees. In this,
and indeed in the work of finding sites and preparing
designs, it is likely that Miss Ingham benefited from the
help of her father, A G Ingham, a recently retired Civil
Engineer. He had become a member of the Dean of Guild
Court and would later be elected Baillie.

That Viewpoint was breaking new ground by
pursuing their case is confirmed by Miss Ingham's report
the following year of a meeting with officials from the
Department of Health for Scotland (DHS), who were

'very interested in this scheme and would like to see it go forward as the Viewpoint Housing Society were *the only people in the country* who had made use of the facilities offered by the Housing Act.[73] By the end of 1953, three sites had been acquired for flats in the Morningside and Grange areas of Edinburgh: at Newbattle Terrace, Findhorn Place at the junction with Grange Loan, and Chalmers Crescent. Getting written agreement for the plans from the DHS proved frustratingly slow but the gratifying outcome of the negotiations with the Local Authority was that the high price of the developments received, as Miss Ingham had anticipated, an eighty per cent loan from the Edinburgh Corporation together with a twenty per cent investment in the Society's funds by purchase of loan stock. This was, in fact, a pioneering example of the kind of mortgage arrangement that in 1957 would be formalised as part of the Housing Act. 'I think they are the only Local Authority in Scotland to invest in any such Society', Miss Ingham told the *Edinburgh Evening News*.[74]

Contemporary reports speak not only of the distinctive method of waste disposal featured in the new flats but also of a communal 'washhouse' on each floor and electrically heated drying cabinets. 'Particular attention has been paid ... to the suppression of noise'. Flats were separated by cavity walls, asphalt was used for the stair treads and the floors were constructed of 'hollow concrete slabs with a half-inch thickness of glass silk, on which is laid a "fully floating" wood floor'.[75] It was possible for the new flats to be heated by gas, electricity or solid fuel. Similarly, kitchenettes were fitted for either gas or electric cookers, and a variety of sockets were installed to suit different household gadgets. Miss Ingham's father, described by the *Edinburgh Evening News* as 'technical man' for the Society, was especially proud of the plumbing arrangements. 'We are pioneering in Edinburgh with the one-stack drainage system ... This avoids having duplicate pipes and, it is claimed, saves £30 - £40 a house in drains.'[76] By providing such accommodation for single women, declared the *Edinburgh Evening Dispatch*, Viewpoint had taken 'the first major step towards the solution of a particular type of housing problem in Edinburgh.'[77]

Despite the fact that, in overall terms, new building by Housing Associations across Britain continued at a very low level up to the end of the 1950s[78], this was the very period in which Viewpoint had made inroads into such work. It was a new stage and a remarkable expansion of Miss Cunningham's original concept. Perhaps with that in mind, Viewpoint now departed from the alphabet series of names, and named the Newbattle Terrace development after Miss Cunningham. In order to get round a legal caveat concerning the building of flats in the area, Viewpoint was advised to describe Cunningham House as a 'hostel with certain communal facilities' – so not quite shaking off the image of the first bed sits. Two years later, Miss Cunningham resigned from 'active participation' in Viewpoint at the age of 79, her legacy now adapting to changing expectations and growing with a new sense of energy and possibility.

Chapter 8
Making a community

From the mid-1950s onwards, the building of new properties would add an important dimension to Viewpoint's work. This was not a cheap option, however, despite the new mortgage-style arrangements now available to the organisation. Rising building costs would affect a number of projects over the coming years, often prolonging the time that they took to arrange and complete. Therefore, Viewpoint also continued down its well-trod path of looking for properties to convert, and over the next fifteen years these two approaches progressed hand in hand.

Equally important were the policy initiatives that the organisation adopted. Some of these were planned in a strategic way, others were not – but each reflected the changing needs and expectations of older people and of society at large. Those at the organisation's helm always regarded these activities and endeavours, if not ahead of their time then, at the very least, forward-looking. 'The name Viewpoint', explained one later publicity brochure, 'covers a wide spectrum of experimental ideas for the comfort and security of elderly people'. One of these ideas was the creation of a Home for older people in Ettrick Road.

Properties were purchased in the Greenhill and Inverleith areas of the city and then, in early 1956, the

Association announced that it had also bought number 12 Ettrick Road, which it intended to convert into seven flats, 'subject to the approval of various official Committees'.[79] By the following September, Miss Ingham was reporting that tenders received for intended conversion were far higher than expected; indeed, over twice the amount received for a similar conversion at Chalmers Crescent. She did not expect to receive approval from the DHS for the £9,000 estimate and suggested that the Committee consider 'dividing the house into two first class flats, each with garage, and then sell on the open market'.[80]

At some point between that September and the following April, however, Miss Ingham changed her mind and came up with a quite different solution to the Ettrick Road problem:

> *The Secretary said that members of Committee would be aware that she felt that No.12 Ettrick Rd should be considered as a possible home for the more elderly of the Societies' [sic] tenants and members. With this in mind she had interviewed various officials of the City, and of DHS, and the National Assistance Board. All had expressed good will for the project, and she felt that if the Committee agreed to start such a scheme, there seemed little doubt but that the necessary finance would be forthcoming.[81]*

The image that this account conjures up, of Miss Ingham doing the interviewing and city officials being called, trembling, to account, more than indicates the sense of confidence and determination she felt in her dealings with Edinburgh's housing and building bodies. To what

'Typing is my one wage-earning accomplishment'. Miss Jane Cunningham in her apartment at Rutland Street

Miss Cunningham in 1962, taking the sleeper from London to Stranraer in her beloved Galloway

Above. 'I had no spirit of play'. The young Jane Cunningham sat apart from the other children in the gardens of Saxe-Coburg Place

Right. Anne House, Viewpoint's first property – the ground floor and basement of 9 Warrender Park Crescent

Above. 'We also had seven rabbit hutches'. The Lady Provost of Edinburgh inspects the kitchen at Anne House

Left. Charlotte House, 203 Newhaven Road – third of the 'alphabet houses'

Single Women Co-operate in 'No-Profit' Housing Plan

The Countess of Elgin looking at some of the gifts received for the bring-and-buy sale in Bridget House, 5 Northumberland Street, Edinburgh, which she opened on Saturday. The house, which has been divided into rooms for single women, is the third to be acquired by the Viewpoint Housing Society, Ltd. (Picture by a staff photographer.)

There are 250 members of the Viewpoint Housing Society, and a waiting list of new members. The Society aims at bringing together those who want homes and those who want to help the housing problem for single women.

The cost of the rooms in Bridget House varies from 17s 6d to 35s a week, depending on size and situation. The price includes hot water, light, gas for cooking, rates and taxes. The occupants of the house share the kitchen. Members of the society went round Bridget House and Charlotte House, 203 Newhaven Road, the other recently-acquired property, to put their names down for the various rooms.

The society is non-profit-making, and the sale was held to defray incidental expenses.

Lady Elgin, who was introduced by Miss J. M. M. Cunningham, chairman of the committee of management, said that, as a member of Fife County Council Housing Committee, she knew well that overcrowding and living in sub-let rooms was the sad lot of so many people just now.

Local Authorities were doing their utmost to rehouse families, but the single woman was having a hard time and had to fend for herself.

The Countess of Elgin attends the bring-and-buy sale at the opening of Bridget House

Left. Ann Evelyn Ingham, Viewpoint's guiding spirit for 40 years.

Below. Miss Ingham at the opening of Ingham Court in 1985

Cleaning the silver at Viewpoint Housing Society's Home for Older Ladies

WORK TO BE DONE
HELP WANTED!

'Residents are encouraged to take on suitable tasks such as silver cleaning.' A publicity brochure for Ettrick Road 'Guest House Home'

A Burns Supper at Ettrick Road

Gillespie Crescent, Viewpoint's first Sheltered House scheme – a drawing by Miss Ingham

THROOM

DELIVERY HATCH, ENTRANE
FUEL STORE

VING ROOM

Innovative designs were a feature of the new flats at Cunningham House

extent this particular solution was Miss Ingham's alone, we don't know. In 1956, she had been elected for a three-year period to the Council of the National Federation of Housing Societies, based in London, and through this and other connections she was no doubt broadening her knowledge of the options open to Housing Societies at this time.

Ettrick Road would become the first of Viewpoint's 'Guest House Homes'. Exactly what this meant is outlined in a leaflet produced in the 1970s to explain and publicise the work of Viewpoint Benevolent. This distinct association was to become the fund raising arm of the organisation as a whole. However, for reasons that soon become clear, the first seed for Viewpoint Benevolent might be said to have been sown with the plans established to support the Ettrick Road project. As later defined, the proposed 'Guest House' was designed for the 'frail elderly, but active retired professional women and widows of professional men, and those familiar with the work of voluntary organisations who share some interests in common'. It was not to be a nursing home – 'chronic illness cannot be handled' – and residents were expected to play a part in the running of the house as well as looking after their own rooms. 'This may be no more than the setting of tables or cleaning silver and certainly those with "green" fingers will find plenty to do with plants and flowers ... all should be willing to help one another.'[82] Guest House living was built around a certain amount of communal activity, including the sharing of meals together, while offering an appropriate degree of independence and privacy.

An undated document, written it seems for the

benefit of a successor as manager at Ettrick Road, gives an extraordinarily vivid description of life in the Guest House and the attempts to give it the feel of a homely (if occasionally understaffed) hotel. It is run, at this time, by a 'Superintendent' and assistant matron:

> *There may be times when, due to staff shortage, help is needed in the kitchen or diningroom or Sick Room and both Superintendent and a[ssistant] matron are asked to see that there is no friction. We realize that this sort of willing service is what makes the difference between a Home and an Institution.*
>
> *The Guest Houses should aim to be small Hotels where nursing and its needs and service are not obtrusive. A House Rule is that illnesses and ailments* shall not *be discussed in the Public Rooms, or with the residents etc.*

The 'Object' of the Ettrick Road ethos is described as creating 'a happy home atmosphere where residents are encouraged to take on suitable tasks such as:- clearing at *end* of meal, and setting up tables, silver cleaning, filling of pepper and salts, sugar bowls, folding paper napkins, looking after plants. These almost have to be *assigned* to suitable residents, and they may need prodding in case these are forgotten.'

A varied regime of meals is laid out. Breakfast is taken in the residents' rooms on trays; 'elevenses' are served in the dining room. Afternoon tea is available at 3.30pm, 'to which visitors may be invited.' The writer comments that: 'Tea is a bit of a nuisance because it calls for home baking, but I hope it can continue.' Of Supper ('a light dinner') she writes:

In the past it was the 'done' thing for residents to change for the evening meal. I'm afraid that this has gone, but I think it is good for them and it is a pity to have the standard dragged down by the few who belong to the 'cardigan' brigade.

Detailed instructions are also offered for how to mark residents' birthdays:

Matron always put a card on breakfast tray (date on next of kin card). 90th birthdays are celebrated with a special meal. Other birthdays – sometimes a resident or friends will give something to the house for their birthday treat and this is usually made known.

The Ettrick Road scheme took some while to progress – a bank interest rise in early January 1958, for example, led to a temporary moratorium on all new work by the Edinburgh Corporation's Finance Committee. But by October the following year work on the refurbishment was progressing well and it was hoped that the house would be ready for residents in March or April. It was also noted that 'the Pleiades group had been over the house.'[83]

Named after the seven sisters of Greek mythology, the Pleiades seems to have been another product of Miss Ingham's fecund imagination – a fund raising group formed expressly to raise money for Ettrick House, and the first formalised attempt to support the costs of furnishing Viewpoint properties. A direct line would lead from this group to the formation of Viewpoint Benevolent, with a great deal more fund raising undertaken along the way.

The new Guest House Home was opened to residents in 1959. First over the threshold was Miss Rankine Brown, the Association's former Chairman. She indicated that she wished to make this move while it was still her own decision, but there was general agreement that having women of her commitment to the organisation in the new Home would help get it up and running. Another such person was Miss E R Craig, the first secretary of George McLeod's Iona Committee. This was, in fact a Home full of remarkable women. Mrs Muir had been a POW in Japan who didn't see her husband again following that experience. And Miriam Young, who came to the Home from a houseboat in India, was known for wearing Tibetan boots in the house.

Other houses were also being purchased or built at this time, each one bringing its own need for compromise or innovation. The new development at Cluny Gardens, opposite the gates leading to Blackford Pond, had to be built as two-storey semi-detached houses in order to fulfil the requirements of the landowner, or 'superior'. In September 1956, the Committee considered acquiring number 6 Bellevue Terrace, expressing a desire to provide some less expensive housing options for the members. The Committee discussed the idea of converting the property into single-room tenancies, each with a private kitchenette, on the same lines as number 15 Northumberland Terrace, but applying for an improvement grant to do it. However, the conversion didn't turn out to be as cost effective as the Committee had hoped. The need to install a system of internal ventilation added considerably to the cost of the work. There was a certain kudos to be gained from this innovative development – official bodies were interested in viewing the results – but Miss Cunningham appeared less than enthusiastic about its financial impact when she addressed the Society's tenth Annual General Meeting in 1957:

> ... the Committee had wished to do very little alteration, but had been forced by the various departments concerned into an elaborate scheme incorporating a new system of induced ventilation for kitchens and bathrooms. While it was satisfactory to know that this scheme was to be regarded as a pilot scheme for all future work of this type in the City, it was disappointing that it would once again prove to be an expensive convertion [sic].[84]

This was an example, noted Miss Cunningham, of how the Society's aim of undertaking cheap conversions, and therefore keeping rents down, was often thwarted by official regulations: 'while the Ministry might indicate that a simpler standard would be accepted, this was not the case.'

The Bellevue development would continue to give cause for concern for some while. The following August, in response to Miss Ingham's update on progress there, Miss Moyse raised the question of the Society's financial burdens – adding, intriguingly, 'at this time of National strain.'[85] Even if Harold Macmillan's recent public optimism ('most of our people have never had it so good') might in hindsight be regarded with some scepticism, it's hard to be precise about what Miss Moyse was referring to. (Ian Penman suggests that she may have been alluding to the resignation earlier in the year of Peter

Thorneycroft as Chancellor of the Exchequer over a cabinet dispute about £50 million. In another famous phrase of the day, Macmillan described the incident as 'a little local difficulty.') Whatever the root of Miss Moyse's unease, the Committee agreed to keep the matter in mind. However, it already had other irons in the fire.

In the same 1957 annual report, Miss Cunningham states that new sites are being investigated, among them sites near Edinburgh city centre, which would be suitable for business women who did not wish to travel a long distance to and from work. Among such properties developed were those in Melgund Terrace and East Claremont Street, both situated less than a mile north of Princes Street. The former site had been compulsorily purchased by the Corporation and passed to the Society for creating housing for single people. Restrictions on the site had made purchase problematic before, but the superiors were said to be supportive of this move and 'approved in the work of the Viewpoint Housing Society'.[86]

This re-assertion of the needs of professional business women, suggests Susan Maclennan, was in line with Viewpoint's original principles. Yet, with a growing portfolio of properties purchased in Edinburgh's New Town and other desirable areas of the city, together with the continued emphasis on 'professional' women, it is worth pausing to ask who, less than ten years after its foundation, was being catered for by Viewpoint. What kind of image was it forming for itself both then and for the future? It's a question sometimes raised by those close to the organisation, aware that as the Housing Association movement developed, Viewpoint retained a character perceived to be distinct and even, on occasions, remote from other comparable Associations.

Indeed, in more recent times, the very use of the term, 'professional' was sometimes seen as working against Viewpoint's best interests. Joan Marshall confirms that it was not a word liked by tenants in the 1980s, and when Sandra Brydon arrived to take up the position of Housing Manager in 1996 she encountered a perception of the organisation as old-fashioned and elitist, too much shaped by the middle-income group from which at least its founders – if not its early tenants – had been drawn.

By purchasing properties in the areas that it did, it is sometimes reasoned, Viewpoint was failing to expose itself to a broad mix of social background. Bob Duff certainly felt the force of that argument when he became Viewpoint's Director in 1992. He was one of those who perceived Viewpoint as having what could be termed a middle-class client group. This, it became clear, was also the view of Scottish Homes and other statutory bodies, a fact that added to the Association's difficulties in accessing government funding at that time.

Viewpoint's difficulty was that it had set out to achieve a very particular goal, at a time when few others were interested, namely to enable older single ladies to remain in or near the areas where they had lived and worked, close to friends, churches and familiar communities. Viewpoint simply went to where interested people were. Woodthorpe, the Supported Housing complex in Colinton, for example, initially attracted mainly tenants from the immediately surrounding area. Nowadays, tenants come from further afield but Colinton was, and to some extent remains, 'an old people's village', according to current tenants Isabella and James Glass – and thus an ideal choice of location for the organisation.

But it was not only the location of Viewpoint's properties that helped foster the 'exclusive' image of the organisation. There was the arguably more fundamental issue of how places in each new residence were allocated. This was a matter taken very seriously during the early years of Viewpoint Committee meetings, despite no discernible accountability within the process by which decisions were reached. The Minute recording the way in which the rooms in Fiona House were allocated, for example, is typical: a simple list of rooms, the number of applicants for each room, and a column naming each selected tenant. 'If any dropped out,' the Minute concludes, 'a room could be offered to Miss A, who had been highly recommended by Dr Laurie, of Carubber's Close Mission.'[87] The selection process for Gillian House a year later offers a few more guidelines:

> *The date of joining the Society was the deciding factor, but where there were several applicants of the same seniority for a room, other factors such as present state of mind, recommendations, whether the Society had already offered a room etc., were taken into account.*[88]

There is, too, an implicit understanding that the process of room allocation was about endeavouring to form a workable community of tenants. An explanatory note is added:

> *Rooms D & E had been let to two friends not so senior as some applicants, because it was felt to be for the general*

good of the house and the Society that two friends should share the kitchenette to D.[89]

The Committee's approach was not without its ups and downs, as the case of Miss A, so highly recommended by Dr Laurie, highlighted. She had indeed been offered a room in Fiona House at 17 shillings and 6 pence a week, which she accepted. But when she came to sign the missive her sister, who came in accompaniment, 'had been so abusive on her behalf that Miss Ellis [the Secretary] had given back £1 against her written renunciation of her share, and she had thereby ceased to be a member of the Society.'[90] A later Minute echoes the Miss Pitbladdo affair. It records that Deborah House 'is not a very happy house at the moment':

Miss G and Miss S are not satisfactory tenants. Miss G had been admitted because of her friendship with Miss G't, but she causes a lot of trouble because of her temper. Miss S ... is not able to look after her own room. She would be better off in a boarding house. We had a petition from the other residents asking us to do something about her as they were afraid she might set fire to the house as she was careless in leaving her electric cooker and kettle on till they got red hot.[91]

To minimise such difficulties, the Committee eventually agreed that all tenants should provide the name of a relative or trustee who would accept responsibility 'in case of difficulty or illness', and the names of two people 'who will say that the applicant is adaptable and able to live in harmony with her neighbours.'[92] When it came to the task of sifting through the applications received for the tenancies in the new flat complexes opened in 1956 and '57, these precautions were further reinforced by the decision to call those applicants who were unknown to the Committee for interview – 'the final decision being left to the Secretary'.[93]

The practice of interviewing prospective tenants continued in an unskilled and un-monitored way for many years, though there is no suggestion that interviewers were anything but conscientious. Mrs Margaret Henderson was one of Viewpoint's interviewers in the 1970s. After her mother-in-law moved into Lennox House, she became a volunteer, initially as part of the rent collecting team at Northumberland Street. It was Miss Ingham who asked her to conduct interviews, under her supervision – 'she was a tower of strength', Margaret says. Like the rent collecting, it was work that she enjoyed hugely. She confirms that a key concern was whether a prospective tenant would fit in with the other women. 'The other ladies would tell me: "You've got to get someone who can play bridge." It didn't always work out that way! But I pride myself that I only made one awful mistake. Someone didn't fit.'

The procedure, and some of the other interviewers, could come over as a little snobbish, but clearly the concern for harmonious community remained at the heart of the interviews. Norman Dunhill believed this to be an important consideration, especially when schemes began to receive men as well as women. He became frustrated by the need to meet local government quotas, acknowledging that Viewpoint's policy was to match a person to a scheme 'if we were allowed to'. It was a policy that would have to change as new legislation and Local Authority priorities began to affect markedly the way all Housing Associations allocated places.[94]

Did this desire for communities without conflict in itself make Viewpoint an exclusive organisation? The black and white photos of smartly dressed older women, the presence of titled and influential supporters, the desire for residents to eat with silver cutlery and for every window to be graced by net curtains: these were undoubtedly a reflection of 'well-meaning women with a tradition they wanted to keep up', as one observer puts it.[95] Miss Inglis, a former matron at Lennox Row and later a resident at the Cameron Park complex, speaks of 'a Cranford touch' and recalls Miss Ingham's insistence on 'everything of the best possible standard – fabrics and china.' Royal Doulton was used for breakfasts; Minton for afternoon tea. Matrons took round the morning paper to everyone.[96] Nevertheless, the reality of these communities was often a good deal more complex than it first seemed.

Describing the Viewpoint approach as 'maternalistic', Henry McIntosh suggests that 'there was an element of impoverishment among many of the ladies, and almost an attempt to prevent that being externally obvious.' The desire for a certain uniformity of appearance was not down to snobbishness, he argues; it was to reduce differentiation and to help all concerned maintain a desirable quality of life. More often than not, beneath the veneer there were straitened circumstances. Artist and former teacher Elspeth Buchanan lives at St Raphael's. She observes that 'some people at Viewpoint are wealthy and some have not had the same advantage', but that members of the Viewpoint staff 'are very good at welding us together into something worthwhile.'

Joan Stephenson's recollection is instructive. She was responsible for re-housing tenants from Viewpoint's property in Greenhill Place, due to be sold. All the ladies had moved apart from one, who seemed unusually reluctant to leave her room. She was, Joan assumed, fairly well off. After all, she owned three nice chests of drawers, an unusual luxury. It turned out, however, that each of these impressive items of furniture had been given her after she left each home in which she had been in service. They were all she owned – 'she hadn't a bean to her name', says Joan, and was only receiving benefits, a fact that Viewpoint staff would not have known or enquired about. Her reluctance to move was out of concern that she would be unable to furnish her new flat. Joan's solution was to ask her if she would like to move to a flat already furnished with a pink carpet and curtains ('We were very lady-like about this') – an offer gratefully received.

It does appear that Viewpoint's forward-looking and determined style was not always best served by its desire to hold tightly both to the letter as well as the spirit of its founding aims. As recently as 1996, its policy of allocating mainstream flats only to women who were beyond child-bearing age was out of step with the most up-to-date legal requirements. This was a policy that had its roots in the society's founding task and was instituted at a time, as Norman Dunhill points out, when 'young women wouldn't think of living on their own anyway'. But by the 1990s, the legal framework for allocating housing places was clearer and, in this area, Viewpoint needed to change

– and did. However, the idea that until this point Viewpoint had catered only for 'rather genteel Edinburgh ladies' was simply wrong, says Marjory Sinclair, who joined the staff in 1977.

Certainly, an inspection of the membership register for the first three years of the Society reveals a remarkably diverse group of people. Occasionally a married woman is listed, or a woman of 'private means'. There are also a number of men – a retired schoolmaster in Nairn, an optician, a joiner and an asphalt sheeter among them. For the most part, however, the Register lists single women with an interest in acquiring a room with Viewpoint. There are those whose work would be termed 'professional' – civil servants and teachers, nurses and a journalist – and there are shop workers. But there is also a wide range of other occupations listed: cashiers, clerks and cooks, a serving maid, a sewing maid and a domestic help, a 'worker in crafts' and a power machinist, two Christian Science practitioners, and a masseuse.[97]

Marjorie herself recalls the wide range of tenants and situations that she had to handle as a warden two and a half decades later, first at the Gillespie Crescent development and then at Ingham Court in the Grange area. There were those, she says, who had been very badly treated and others with hygiene issues. She speaks of tenants suffering with TB (though taking tenants with the disease was, at that time, against Viewpoint regulations) and having to facilitate the first 'sectioning' of a tenant that Viewpoint had had to deal with. One formidable GP, whose unforgiving demeanour belied the good medical care he in fact provided, told Marjory that 'these people should be put onto the street. It's the natural order'. Such an attitude was anathema to Viewpoint – but perhaps it indicates that, notwithstanding the use of the term 'professional' and the large number of 'desirable residences' opened by the organisation, the social range of the Society's tenants has always been a good deal greater than might at first have been perceived.

Towards the end of the 1950s, the Committee was on the look-out for new offices for the society. Suitable accommodation was found at number 63 Northumberland Street, previously the manse of St Giles' Cathedral. The building, purchased in 1960, provided Viewpoint's office accommodation for the next thirty years, together with a basement for social and fund raising events.

The following year, a new Housing Act was passed and, once again, Miss Ingham was alert to the advantages open to Viewpoint within the legislation. This 1961 Act, developed by Harold Macmillan's Conservative government, set out to counter the notion that there were only two types of housing available – houses to purchase or council-owned housing for rent, 'with little or no choice for those who did not fit, or did not want to fit, into either tenure.'[98] The Government came to see that Housing Associations were in a position to stimulate unsubsidised private renting. It launched what it regarded as an experiment, making loans available 'to approved non-profit making housing associations which are prepared to build houses to let at economic rents.'[99] This 'pump-priming operation' established a loan fund of £25 million for England and Wales and an additional £3 million for Scotland. It was to this fund that Miss Ingham now turned her attention.

Though the Government had intended that existing Housing Associations would be able to take advantage of the new funds, in practice it became necessary to form new societies. 'One explanation for this is that existing charitable associations were precluded from providing for people who could afford cost rents. Another view ... is that existing associations were too set in their ways or not interested.'[100] Neither of these scenarios applied to Viewpoint and Miss Ingham was anything but uninterested. Indeed, when Peter Malpass observes that the 1961 scheme (which was extended in 1964 with the formation of the Housing Corporation) heralded a 13-year period of considerable growth for housing associations in general, he could very well be referring to Viewpoint in particular.

Viewpoint took advantage of the increased government subsidy to offset the costs of its most ambitious project to date – Cameron Park. Located on the south side of Edinburgh, and nowadays conveniently close to the Cameron Toll shopping centre, the complex was made up of 48 flats and six lock-ups. This scheme, with its distinctively 1960s Scottish appearance derived from a mix of sand-stone, harling and some green lead roofing, was completed in 1965.

Another project with a long gestation period was the residence in Lennox Row, located in the Trinity area and just a stone's throw from the Forth. This project continued the work begun 'almost unintentionally' at Ettrick Road. Publicity for Ettrick Road had spoken of 'the urgent need of the current period' to provide suitable accommodation for the aged 'where some care and attention may be given'. Its one-time matron, Miss

Inglis, described the goal as 'gracious living for older people.'[101] This extension of Viewpoint's commitment was reinforced when a new wing was later added to the Ettrick Road property in order to accommodate the 'frail elderly'. For the moment, the new sphere of care was taken up at number 22 Lennox Row, first viewed in 1963 but not opened until five years later, complete with a newly constructed extension added to the original stone villa. Representing a capital investment of £83,000, this was the first home entirely equipped with single rooms and, although residents had to share bathroom facilities, each had their own wash-hand basin. Although Lennox Row was not designed as a Nursing Home, full nursing facilities were made available for residents and bedside alarm bells were installed. 'Should residents have to go to hospital at any time their place in the Homes will be kept for them', read one report of the opening. The residence was located in spacious grounds and included a sun lounge as one of its attractions. Such was the interest in the development that it received over one thousand visitors during the customary viewing week.

Also popular was the first of Viewpoint's 'Residential Clubs' established in Inverleith Terrace, with views across to Edinburgh's Royal Botanic Gardens. The concept was similar to that of the Guest House Homes – an option for older ladies who wished to retain their independence but who 'needed to be free of household responsibilities.'[102] As at Ettrick Road and Lennox Row, residents had their own private living accommodation but took their meals in a communal dining room. The key difference was that Residential Clubs were not intended for the frailest elderly. Instead, they were seen as offering 'a new lease of life to many and for others ... a happy transitional stage before Guest House or medical nursing home."[103]

The Inverleith Terrace development was faced with a number of delays caused by a steep increase in building costs as well as a strike by builders. By the time it was opened, in 1973, Viewpoint had undergone a number of significant changes in its organisation. In 1968, in order to comply with new legislation, the 'Society' became Viewpoint Housing Association, allowing it to be registered with the Housing Corporation and become eligible to receive grants and loans towards building new housing. Equally important was the split created in 1972 between the Association and a separate entity, the Viewpoint Benevolent Association – both having charitable status.

Viewpoint Benevolent took on responsibility for managing the Guest House Homes, Residential Clubs and the earliest houses such as Bridget and Charlotte but, in addition, 'Benevolent' was committed to fund raising for additional amenities. Benevolent was an outworking of the Pleiades and other initiatives (Chapter 9), and a precursor to the Viewpoint Trust that would be established later. It was able to handle donations and bequests, dispersing them on behalf of Viewpoint Housing Association, which Norman Dunhill describes as being (unlike Viewpoint Benevolent) 'semi-controlled by government.'

With the arrival of Norman Dunhill at Viewpoint in 1975, and the appointment of Joan Stephenson as Housing Manager, Miss Ingham (who in 1963 had been awarded the MBE for her endeavours at Viewpoint) took on the role of Secretary of Viewpoint Benevolent. Norman, meanwhile, set about driving forward Viewpoint's next big initiative, the development of Sheltered Housing. Together, Miss Ingham and Norman Dunhill were a formidable partnership. Under their leadership, Viewpoint exuded a renewed sense of energy, expanding the number of residential places under its management, and fund raising as never before.

Chapter 9
The importance of fund raising

From its earliest days, fund raising was one of Viewpoint's core activities; for many it became the cornerstone of their involvement with the Association. In particular, the large-scale fairs and coffee mornings, held at Edinburgh's Assembly Rooms and in the grounds of George Heriot's School in the 1970s and 80s provide some of the happiest memories for many who have worked with the organisation. Significant amounts of money were raised at such events, as in the pioneering charity shops opened by Viewpoint over the years. But even (and perhaps especially) at smaller events – the continuous round of coffee mornings, whist drives and other fund raising initiatives – this fundamental aspect of Viewpoint's work had the effect of drawing people together. For residents, tenants, staff and volunteer supporters alike, the companionship derived from fund raising activities was not only invaluable – it was the source of their unstinting loyalty to an organisation that often became central to their lives.

The tradition of holding viewing days prior to the opening of new houses has already been noted, as have the 'bring and buy' sales that accompanied these events and which raised funds to purchase fittings and items of furnishing. In the early days, this was the only way a house could be made comfortable and suitably equipped for its new tenants. There was also a sense in which the viewing day sales set a model for new residents – establishing an expectation that they, too, would do their bit to raise the necessary funds for an organisation that did everything on a shoestring. 'The donation from Eleanor House, the proceeds of a whist drive arranged by Miss Bain, was reported to the Committee', reads the Minute of April 28, 1952, 'and it was agreed to write a letter appreciating this gesture [*sic*]. The chairwoman told the Committee that originally this money had been intended for deckchairs and a watering can, and she asked that the Committee should agree to pay for at least a watering can. The suggestion met with approval.'

Once appointed Secretary to Viewpoint in 1952, it didn't take Miss Ingham long to start thinking of ways in which the money raised by such efforts could be consolidated. In June that year, she raises the idea of 'some type of benevolent fund within the framework of the Society', having already borrowed a trial Deed from the Housing Federation. This she proposes showing to the Society's solicitor, Mr Cheyne, for comment.[104] It is not clear whether that idea comes to anything immediately but at the 1955 AGM, there is the announcement of a 'Common Fund', open for donations, bequests and revenue from sales of work, coffee mornings and other similar activities.[105]

Eventually, it was Viewpoint Benevolent that would become the main recipient and distributor of donated income but, in the meantime, the Pleiades group was established in April 1957 with the express purpose of raising funds for the proposed 'Guest House' at Ettrick Road. The idea was to recruit up to 250 people, each of whom would subscribe £1 a year. 'This would be preferable to raising funds by Sales of Work etc'. The name was chosen on the grounds that, in astronomy, the Pleiades were described as 'a conspicuous' cluster of stars within a great number of others.[106] In the event, the newly created group promptly set about organising two coffee parties, instigated by Miss Ingham. It was a success, and by the following January, the Pleiades account stood at £368.00. Also at Miss Ingham's suggestion, her mother was invited to take charge of what is now referred to as a 'Society', and to look after its finances.

A newsletter from 1959 suggests the considerable effort being put into raising funds and the extent to which the extended Viewpoint 'family', as well as the wider community, was being drawn into the voluntary movement. Two appeal funds were running, both designed to raise money for the Ettrick Road project. 10,000 copies of one leaflet were to be issued, to be followed up by an advertisement in *The Scotsman*.[107] In addition, an Easter Market was being planned for the following year with a variety of stalls and evening entertainment, the organisation for which was immense.

However, another item was reported which highlights the Viewpoint ethos of not simply providing bricks and mortar, but also of encouraging friendship and promoting entertainment among its members. A club room and canteen for about 40 people had been opened in the basement at Number 6 Bellevue Terrace, one of the properties acquired for letting. Members were invited to organise a morning or afternoon tea or coffee party, whist drive or bridge drive to help raise funds. Indeed, the club room was to be opened on Christmas Day and New Year's Day for the exchange of greetings. As Miss Ingham summed up in her letter:

As you know, when we all became members of Viewpoint we did something more than just put our names on a piece of paper. We became a family and so strong is the expression and love in family life, that now, as in any smaller family when a new need arises, the whole family is joining together in mutual service for the well being of those less able to take the strain.

Within Viewpoint there was from the beginning a recognition that money would have to be spent with real care, that nothing should be wasted and that much would have to be found second-hand or through donations. Joan Marshall recalls Miss Ingham buying up second-hand household items, silver cutlery for example, that might come in useful. Typically, Miss Cockburn reported an advertisement for second-hand chairs – suitable perhaps for helping to furnish the Bellevue property – and Miss Ingham agreed to enquire about them.[108] The same Minute reports that letters had been sent out, with mixed results, to carpet manufacturers asking if they had any 'seconds' for sale. One firm had replied, referring Viewpoint to 'a good friend in Edinburgh, who turned out to be C&J Brown of Newington' – evidently a good thing.

The business of acquiring second-hand goods turned almost accidentally into the business of selling them when, in late 1962, a fund raising shop was started up in the basement of the offices at 63, Northumberland Street. A quantity of second-hand clothes, which had been gathered for a jumble sale that was subsequently cancelled, was brought to the office and sold instead from there. The Minutes of December 19 that year record that 'this had proved to be of great benefit to some tenants; one going to America to take up domestic work had been able to kit herself out, even to shoes for "difficult feet".[109]

The 'shop' became known as 'Petticoat Lane' and over the years a small bank of volunteers (all trained, co-incidentally, in areas of social work) dispensed advice as well as making money for Viewpoint. Indeed, it was not until February 1984 that Petticoat Lane finally ceased to operate, when its original Convener, Miss C B Ramsay, retired. Reports of the shop's annual coffee morning appear regularly in the Minutes, and in 1967 it was reported that 'the Lane' had raised £2,000 for new carpets at Lennox Row, over which one thousand people had walked during the course of the viewing week.

Throughout the 1960s, coffee mornings, bazaars and sales continued unabated, now supported by radio and television appeals, themselves partly funded by monthly coffee parties held in the Viewpoint office for friends and members. The broadcast appeals were made on Viewpoint's behalf by Miss Ingham herself,[110] the Revd Dr Leonard Small (Moderator of the General Assembly of the Church of Scotland in 1966 and known as 'the radio padre') and actor Gordon Jackson (at that time most well-known for his Ealing film roles and for playing the admirer of arguably Edinburgh's most famous single, professional lady – Miss Jean Brodie). The 1962 radio appeal was intended to raise funds for the Lennox Row development but, as a newsletter from this period said: 'There is still a long way to go before that is achieved and so in addition to whist drives and bridge parties there will be a biennial Easter Market in March.'

The Easter Markets were held in the Assembly

Rooms on George Street. Photos show them to have been big and bustling affairs. The early Markets were lengthy affairs, beginning at 10am and not ending until 9.30pm in order to take full advantage of the day hire and also to accommodate those who were at work during the day. As well as the expected array of baking, bric-a-brac and fancy goods stalls, from 10am there was a coffee morning, while from 2.30pm whist drives, bridge drives and fashion shows were held. The evening would be given over to a Café Chantant, with entertainers such as the well-known Newhaven Fisherwomen's Choir. The whole event was staffed by an army of volunteers under the direction of the Committee and Secretary, who in 1966 'stumped around all day in plaster from a fractured ankle'. The Easter Market was revived in 1988, once again to raise funds for Lennox Row – this time extension and upgrading works. The turnout was reported as being overwhelming, raising a sum of £6,000. The amounts raised at the earlier events were also impressive, but not enough to meet Viewpoint's more costly ambitions.

The costs for establishing residential homes were high and fund raising progress slow. By 1966, Miss Ingham was investigating the option of fund raising professionally and took advice from a firm of consultants, which resulted in an Appeal Committee being set up. It included Lord Balfour of Burleigh, Lord Roseberry and Dr Small, together with Lady Avonside who would later serve as a Chair of Viewpoint. One result was a full-page appeal the following year in the *Edinburgh Tatler* by Lord Dalkeith, the Committee's chairman. It marked, he said, the 21st anniversary of an organisation that was currently helping 'some 350 ladies in one way or another':

The latest project – a new residential home in Lennox Row, represents a capital investment of some £83,000. To provide furnishings and equipment for this home, voluntary effort had already raised £10,000. This considerable sum covers gifts from the 'Petticoat Lane' shop (run by voluntary helpers) to proceeds of our radio appeal and help from the Sembal Trust. It is impossible to evaluate the voluntary help of all kinds that we receive and upon which we depend but it is now necessary to support this effort by a major building appeal.[111]

It was hoped that the efforts of this 21st anniversary year would lead to the completion of Lennox Row and in this way mark 'a turning point' in the organisation's development. The property did indeed open in June of that year but though the total income for the year rose considerably, the Society failed to achieve the bonanza that it had hoped for. Miss Ingham, never wholly convinced of the value of professional fund raisers, therefore returned to the tried and tested methods of Assembly Room markets, coffee mornings and whist drives.

This didn't mean that Viewpoint gave up entirely on major appeals. The Queen's Silver Jubilee in 1977 also marked Viewpoint's own 25th anniversary, and the Silver Jubilee Appeal (also known as 'the Elizabeth Fund') was launched for funds to build extensions and amenities for the organisation's Sheltered Housing. Viewpoint could obtain grants for building but not for carpets or furnishings. A brochure was produced expressing 'deep appreciation of Her Majesty's selfless service to the people of this country' and inviting anyone who shared one of the Queen's three names to make a donation to

Viewpoint. (Though, oddly, the Queen's second name was given inaccurately as 'Louise'.)

One new venture resulting from the 1967 push was a budget shop, opened at Tanfield, Canonmills for the sale of bric-a-brac and nearly new clothes and staffed by volunteers until its closure in 1992. At a time when charity shops were far less common than nowadays, the Tanfield shop was in its way another pioneering Viewpoint effort. Under the guidance of Mrs Etta Whyte, it was the first and most successful of a number of charity shops opened by the Association over the years, proving itself to be one of the central pillars of the organisation's fund raising efforts.

> One of the most successful ways of making money for charity today [reported *The Glasgow Herald*] is not to have your volunteers sewing tea cosies or knitting quietly at home but to organise them into running a shop. And particularly the sort that specialise in good-quality second-hand clothes.
>
> Entering solidly into the business fray – they already have one semi-shop in Edinburgh called Petticoat Lane, that opens for half a day a week and has raised nearly £3,000 – is the appeal committee of the Viewpoint Housing Society ... The row of suits, in a variety of colours and sizes, would have done justice to many a non-second-hand dress shop. The idea is to keep prices low and quality high. Their only problem at the moment is not sales – they have had so many inquiries prior to opening – but keeping up stocks.[112]

Describing how she got involved in this enterprise, Etta Whyte is one of many former Viewpoint volunteers who simply alludes to the fact that Miss Ingham 'had a way ... '. She went along to a meeting in the 'dungeon' basement at Northumberland Street, 'and that was that'. The Tanfield shop was located near the former paper mill on the banks of the Water of Leith. (On one occasion, recalls Etta, thieves used the river as a convenient location for dumping bags from which they had stolen the shop's takings.) Over the years the shop offered that sense of 'family' that many associate with the leadership of Miss Ingham and Norman Dunhill. Its success has already been noted in Miss Ingham's thank you letter to Etta. Between 1968 and 1992, £144,470 was donated to Viewpoint – average annual takings of just over £7,000. This income was recognised as making 'an enormous contribution to our success and to the wellbeing of our residents and tenants'[13] but by 1991, when Etta was looking to retire, questions arose about how and whether to continue the enterprise. No other volunteer wished to take over her coordinating role and the property itself was becoming costly to maintain, partly because of occasional flooding problems resulting from its proximity to the river. And so, following her retirement, the shop closed.

Nevertheless, the Tanfield shop had set a precedent. Other shorter-lived shops were established that added an element of good-natured competition to the retail endeavours. As Ian Penman notes, in the late 1970s and '80s, the Government laid a good deal of emphasis on the need for Housing Associations to do their own fund raising. 'Viewpoint could get Brownie points from the regulator for having shops and so forth'. Indeed, such was their success that, in the mid 1980s, the Inland Revenue insisted that Viewpoint register a trading company for its Budget shop activities: Benview Trading Ltd. 'This company will then covenant its profits back to the Benevolent, thus saving tax', explained Miss Ingham – adding: 'Silly, isn't it?'[114] Benview Trading was incorporated on March 28, 1985, and a card and gift shop was opened at 1 Viewforth Gardens in Bruntsfield under the auspices of the new company. It was managed by the artistic Lesley Stothers, but it proved difficult to sustain this effort. More successful over the long term was the shop opened in Stockbridge and run by Muriel (Peggy) Home, the wife of Professor George Home, Viewpoint Chairman from 1997.

Peggy Home's chief goal was to support the work at St Raphael's Hospital in the Grange, which became part of Viewpoint in the late 1980s. Her association with the institution went back for more than a decade. She had been greatly impressed by the care she received while undergoing an operation there in 1972 and, with George, became a committed fund raiser and supporter for the organisation. Peggy took pleasure in galvanizing friends and neighbours to find replacement curtains and bed linen, and to provide supplies for the trolley of small gifts that she would push round the wards on a weekly basis. But with the shop, she took the fund raising to quite another level.

It was opened next to Viewpoint's property in St Stephen Place (Peggy persuaded a friendly Marks & Spencer manager to lend her mannequins for dressing the window) and on its first day took £450.00. Over the years, the Stockbridge shop gave a total of £27,937.00 to St Raphael's, as well as additional amounts to other charities.

It was a significant achievement, underlined in 1995 when Peggy and her team were singled out for recognition by Volunteer Development Scotland during that year's Volunteer Week.

At around the same time that Peggy and George were putting their energies into fund raising for St Raphael's, a small bric-a-brac shop was being established within what became known as the '100 Club', a ground floor property in Patrick Square acquired by Viewpoint in 1975 and nowadays part of Warners Solicitors.[115] Essentially, however, this was a place for meeting friends, open from ten 'til five. 'If the club is open five days a week', it was calculated, 'and each of the hundred members attends once per week with two friends, that means sixty persons a day and that is probably a comfortable number considering the size of the premises.' Here, members could attend painting and craft classes, use the reading room, or join in organising fund raisers and social events – all of this presided over by another Viewpoint stalwart, Edward French.

Edward French had been a milliner, whose shop on Rose Street had been close to Miss Ingham's own. Described as 'very arty', he was also known for his kindness and sense of fun. He put his professional skills to good use for Viewpoint (an 'Autumn Hat Show' in the early 1970s was one successful fund raiser for the Society) but also drew on city-wide contacts. Through his friendship with notable musician Eric von Ibler, for instance, Edward arranged a fund raising concert by von Ibler's much respected Schola Cantorum of Edinburgh. A charity production of *Princess Ida* by Edinburgh Savoy Opera was also mounted in Leith Town Hall, to which members of Viewpoint staff, dressed in period costume, were driven by horse and carriage. At such events, Edward French was no back-room boy. He was a man who liked to be up on stage when possible, part of the show. A Christmas Concert in 1982, in aid of new Sheltered Housing at Prestonfield, featured Edinburgh musical luminaries, Alan and Jane Borthwick with friends. Edward French is listed in the programme – cover artwork by one, Miss A.E. Ingham – as compère.

It was Edward French who began organising coach trips for Viewpoint members on a regular basis. They were not a new idea. In June 1952, a bus was chartered for a tour of the Borders, instigated by an informal meeting of members interested in organising social events – but this appears to have been a one-off arrangement. In the first instance, Mr French arranged trips for members of the 100 Club but later he responded to interest from other Viewpoint complexes. After his death in 1985, the tradition of coach tours was maintained by Alistair Macintosh, Miss K B Young (a part-time warden at Drummond Place) and others. Some of these trips were day outings, but longer tours were organised, including week-long holidays at Christmas and Hogmanay. In the 1990s, Ann Neil was employed to run a 'Tours Department', a non profit-making service that could offer a high level of volunteer support not available to professional travel agents.[116] 'Truly this innovative service, which receives charitable support from Viewpoint Trust, enhances the quality of residents lives and is of particular benefit to frailer residents who, if the service was not available, would be unable to go on holiday alone.'[117] After Ann Neil left the organisation in 1997, the service was gradually scaled back and, in recent years, demand diminished also.

Fund raising in the 1980s was dominated by the £1 Million Target Fund, set up to try to raise money for a new Residential Home. It was an ambitious project designed to support ambitious plans for what Viewpoint described as 'a new concept of care'. This was a response to the widening gap between the numbers of older people in need of long-term care and the space available for them. The situation, it was argued, had been aggravated by a change of policy by the Hospital Service Administration, which was returning people home following treatment, 'too often to unsuitable surroundings and the same difficulties which brought them to Hospital in the first place'.[118] Viewpoint envisaged:

> ... a Village concept, however small, with coffee shop and boutiques staffed by voluntary workers, where the pace is geared to that of the residents. In addition, a safe environment is proposed for the mildly confused or forgetful, where individuals can go in and out to a safe garden at will ... Also included in our plan are special facilities for the handicapped – something we have lacked until now. It is our deep desire that no one should have to leave us, unless at their own wish or because Hospital treatment is indicated.[119]

At that time, Viewpoint was unable to carry out its plans on such an imaginative scale, but the vision inspired a huge range of fund raising activities – from the sale of marmalade to concerts, sponsored marathons and parachute jumps – and the concept itself has resurfaced in recent times.

Fund raising was in some respects a question of tradition. Three biennial Summer Fairs were held (the first in 1979) in the grounds of George Heriot's School – successors to the Easter Markets. Each had its own theme (Old Time Fayre Brigadoon, Carousel), raised considerable amounts of money, and as usual relied on the goodwill and generosity of tenants, volunteers and office staff who were allocated or gently bullied into volunteering their services by Miss Ingham and Edward French. But no Viewpoint tradition was so grand, so engrained or organised with such military precision as the Christmas Fair, held annually at the Assembly Rooms on George Street.

The event began in 1968 and seems to embody that distinctive mix of money-making and socialising so important to Viewpoint. It was not, strictly speaking, a fund raiser at all but a 'coffee party' or 'at home' for Viewpoint tenants and friends. Tenants were invited to attend without charge (although in the early days a book of raffle tickets was sent with the invitation) and friends paid a small sum. It was, says Joan Marshall, Miss Ingham's way of saying 'Merry Christmas' to all Viewpoint's tenants and was funded by money raised at the Christmas Hypermarket for charities held each November, also in the Assembly Rooms. The Hypermarket was a hugely popular Edinburgh event, organised by the Edinburgh Volunteer Organisations Council (EVOC). Joan recalls queuing from 6a.m. on several cold March mornings outside the EVOC offices in order to get a prime spot for the Viewpoint stall eight months later.

The Viewpoint Christmas event grew over the years to such an extent that over one thousand people could be expected to arrive at the Assembly Rooms – all of them queuing up, so it seemed, before the doors were even opened. The coffee party was designed to feel special. An annual exhibition was organised – of painting or photography one year, of pottery or patchwork quilts the next. A choir would be booked, a commissionaire organised and local schoolgirls 'volunteered' to help. Tables, crockery and silver table candelabras were all hired from Andrew Wilson and Sons Ltd ('By appointment to Her Majesty the Queen, Catering Equipment Hirers'). A list of equipment gathered for the day offers an inkling of the scale of the event:

> *tea cups and saucers*
> *ash trays*
> *sugar bowls*
> *12 cream jugs*
> *wooden trays*
> *tea spoons*
> *12 thermal urns*
> *red candles*
> *candelabras (three-branch)*
> *tables (three foot 'slim fold')*

And refreshments:

> *750 mince pies*
> *loaves made into sandwiches*
> *15lbs of biscuits*
> *6 lbs of chocolates*

box of tea bags (40 people had tea)
gallons of milk
coffee (Melrose's)
brown sugar

– not forgetting 24 chocolate oranges. For one thousand people?

Susan Maclennan describes the event: 'The chandeliers in the Assembly Rooms twinkled, the smell of rarely-worn fur coats and hats filled the air. The noise level of a thousand older people talking was astonishing, and the choir sang in the background. Doors were manned to ease the stampede and local tradesmen asked to assist with washing up and carrying heavy urns ... It was a chance to meet old friends and welcome new, and to enjoy seeing the Viewpoint family together.'

Margaret Henderson recalls that the events were hard work but always enjoyable. 'I remember being part of a team that made 1,000 sandwiches in a single afternoon!' And after it was all over, Miss Ingham sat down (as well she might) and wrote numerous personal letters to helpers, volunteers and staff, thanking them all, in her own inimitable way, for their help. The work done by volunteers and staff alike on occasions such as these was vital, but it was personal too – a fact that Miss Ingham never forgot. Whole families and whole Viewpoint houses and schemes got involved. Volunteering underpinned the 'family' ethos of the organisation. As times moved on, it became increasingly difficult to maintain that ethos. The Viewpoint Trust perhaps engendered a formality to fund raising that hadn't been there previously; Viewpoint itself was moving towards a more business-like model of operation.

As Viewpoint began its slow transformation into the modern housing and care organisation that it is today, it is perhaps too easy simply to associate the 'old Viewpoint' with shoe-string endeavours and hand-to-mouth fund raising events, with their teams of sandwich makers and stylish touches of decoration. Undoubtedly this was all part of the Viewpoint way, but at the same time, 'old-style' social pioneers such as Miss Ingham were perpetually on the look-out for new opportunities and possibilities. It was Miss Ingham who pushed Viewpoint Benevolent into the computer age in 1981, several years before the Association would take up such new-fangled technology. A full decade passed before Joan Marshall, sent round the corner to purchase that first computer from a friendly neighbourhood shop, was asked by the Association's Housing Officers to create a system for them that could hold details of current and prospective tenants.

The tug-of-war between the old ways and the new would be an increasingly marked characteristic of Viewpoint's development over the ensuing years: new systems, new policies, new legislation. Yet, it's still possible to say that Viewpoint's ability to remain active and growing sixty years after its foundation is vibrant proof of what can be achieved on the back of goodwill and a coffee morning.

Chapter 10
Breaking new ground

In 1974, Norman Dunhill was appointed as a consultant to Viewpoint. The following year, he became the Association's first Director. Norman's arrival coincided with significant developments in government housing policy that would have far-reaching consequences for Housing Associations. Most especially, Norman's key task over the coming years would be to take advantage of new legislation that facilitated the building of sheltered accommodation. Joan Stephenson, appointed as Housing Manager in 1975, describes this period as a time of considerable excitement. It saw Viewpoint not only grow considerably in size but also in its range of service delivery. 'There was a sense of pushing the boat out in this period,' Joan recalls, though it wouldn't be long before Viewpoint's ambitions were being hampered by ever-tightening financial constraints.

Norman was a man of considerable energy and determination, more than equal to Miss Ingham's own unquenchable enthusiasms. He had moved to Scotland in 1959 to work in the Housing and Research Unit of Edinburgh University, at which time he first met Miss Ingham – still serving on the council of the National Federation of Housing Associations and a prominent figure in the Scottish housing scene. Subsequently Norman was appointed as the Housing Corporation's man in Scotland but he returned eventually to the university and, at Miss Ingham's instigation, was drawn gradually into the workings of Viewpoint. He describes it as being run by Miss Ingham with the support of one office worker and a committee. She needed help in the changing legislative climate, and he was looking for a challenge. His involvement with Viewpoint was mutually beneficial.

Viewpoint was, by comparison with other housing organisations, 'tiny'. It was, says Jack Fleming, a somewhat 'hand-knitted kind of organisation.' Jack would become Chairman of Viewpoint but, like Norman Dunhill, already had knowledge of the organisation while Assistant Secretary in the Scottish Development Department and later as Secretary of the Scottish Special Housing Association. He saw a need, observes Ian Penman, 'to sort things out a bit without upsetting the old ladies or doing violence to the Viewpoint tradition.' Joan Marshall, who joined Viewpoint four years after Norman, reinforces this impression of a rather less than organised approach to the business of housing. She had been taken on in order to support Miss Ingham's own assistant, Miss Grant, though precisely what her responsibilities were was not entirely clear. Work, she says, came in fits and starts – it was a continual situation of feast or famine.

By the time Norman Dunhill joined the staff, Viewpoint had already built up a substantial stock of housing, an achievement noted by Joan Stephenson when invited to address residents and staff at Inverard House on the occasion of Viewpoint's 50th anniversary in 1997.

> By 1972, Viewpoint was 25 years old and had over 300
> flats. And equally important, by 1972, after years of
> campaigning, government thinking was changing. The
> work of Housing Associations, with their enormous
> voluntary effort, was recognised and grants became
> available for building. I just can't tell you how exciting it
> was ... This really was a time for dreams to come true.
> Norman Dunhill joined the organisation, committees
> became more formal, and he and Miss Ingham began to
> negotiate the minefield of rules and regulations set up to
> ensure that no penny of government money would be
> wasted.[120]

The 'minefield' that Joan refers to resulted in part from
the Housing Finance Act of 1972, 'one of the most contro-
versial pieces of housing legislation since 1945.'[121] The
legislation revolved around two key principles: that rents
would be set not by local councillors or Housing
Association boards but by independent rent officers, and
that existing government subsidies (excepting those to
Housing Associations for improvement and conversion)
would be withdrawn over ten years. In their place, a
temporary new-building subsidy was enacted.

The new system, writes Peter Malpass:

> exposed associations to considerable risk and uncer-
> tainty, in the sense that on the one hand they faced the
> prospect of phased subsidy withdrawal while on the
> other hand the fair rent system (with rents set externally
> by independent rent officers) meant that they [had] no
> freedom to adjust rentals to match spending commit-
> ments.[122]

The legislation was complicated. Not only were Housing Associations required to register fair rents for all their dwellings within three and a half months of the Act coming into force; in addition, 'the new subsidies introduced in the Act were difficult to understand and operate, and they had a strongly deterrent effect on new building'.[123]

The 1972 Housing Finance Act proved so contentious and so difficult to operate that it lasted only 18 months and had been withdrawn by the time Norman Dunhill arrived at Viewpoint. Nevertheless, it wasn't for nothing that he and Miss Ingham sometimes felt that the rules were made to prevent them building anything.[124] Gradually, however, as Joan Stephenson described, the tide was turning in favour of Housing Associations. Through the 1970s and into the early 80s they developed more rapidly south of the border than in Scotland, but there was growing dissatisfaction even in Scotland with Local Authority provision of housing, and pressure to develop the role of Housing Associations here as well. Associations brought to the sector, Ian Penman believes, the framework and guarantees of state regulation, some minimum standards for building, and a degree of enterprise.[125]

The start of a sea change in the fortunes of Housing Associations as a whole can be linked to the 1974 Housing Act that followed hard on the heels of the failed 1972 legislation. Though this Act had been prepared under the Conservatives, it was under the new Labour Government that it passed into law. It reinforced the decline of private renting in favour of Housing Associations. There were doubts, notes Peter Malpass, about the 'competence and capacity' of the Associations (until this point rather minor players in the social housing sector as a whole) to 'expand into a significant force'.[126] However, in retrospect the Act represents the point at which the Housing Association movement as it exists today really took off, with a focus on rehabilitation and special needs.[127] Although the Act did not make it a statutory duty of Local Authorities to involve associations, subsequent Department of Environment circulars made it quite clear that cooperation was expected (as had already been achieved by the Edinburgh Council and Viewpoint) and that Housing Associations could no longer be ignored.

First as a consultant, then as Director, Norman Dunhill was charged with taking full advantage of the 1974 Housing (Scotland) Act, and the chief advantage that he saw was the opportunity it encouraged to develop Sheltered Accommodation. Already the 300 units owned by Viewpoint offered varying degrees of support to residents, so that when Housing Corporation loans became available for Sheltered Housing as a result of the Government's new drive, 'we were halfway or more geared up for it and were able to take up Sheltered Housing in a big way'.[128] As early as September 11, 1975, Lord Goodman, the Chairman of the Housing Corporation, cut the first sod and laid the foundation stone for what was one of the very first Sheltered Housing schemes to be built under the provisions of the 1974 Act.

Gillespie Crescent, with upwards of 200 places, had the feel of a small village. It was a mixed development on a two and a half acre site, combining flats, designed for older people able to lead a fully independent life

(Wright's House), and Sheltered Housing (Gillespie House). Standard regulations required that bed-sitting rooms should lead off from an arrangement of corridors, but Viewpoint was aiming higher and – in Wright's House – stuck by its determination to create two and three-bedroom flats. Gillespie House, meanwhile, was advertised as 'an arrangement of grouped self-contained flats for those older people who are able to maintain an independent existence with some support plus main meal'. These flats were arranged in two groups of four storeys, with limited services initially – central heating, garden maintenance and an alarm system. But again, Viewpoint intended to raise the game beyond minimum statutory requirements. 'In every case application has been made for Fair Rent. It is however the intention of Viewpoint to form a services and amenities association here as on other sites at an additional charge. Once this is in operation it should be possible to provide a consid-erable increase in the services offered.'[129]

Located just to the west of Bruntsfield Links, the Gillespie Crescent properties took names that reflected the history of the area. James Gillespie, an eighteenth century merchant and snuff manufacturer, had bequeathed money for the foundation of a charitable hospital and workshop for the elderly, and a free school for the education of poor boys (now James Gillespie's High School). The ownership of the workshop eventually passed to the Royal Blind Asylum Workshops, from whom Viewpoint acquired the site. 'Thus it returns in some measure to Gillespie's purpose', read the early publicity, 'and it is fitting that the Sheltered Housing planned for this group should be called Gillespie House.'

Perhaps Viewpoint felt it needed to pull public opinion back on side following 'the astonishment of many Edinburgh citizens' that the famous old Gillespie's Hospital building had been demolished 'almost overnight to make way for the building of small flats for old people.'[130] The name Wright's House, meanwhile, is taken from the mansion-house that originally stood on the site ('Wrychtishousis').[131] The name is shared with the small lane adjacent to the Links, the site of the oldest extant golf clubhouse in Scotland – nowadays 'Ye Olde Golf Tavern.'

It was for Gillespie Crescent that Viewpoint advertised for 'a mature lady with experience of the elderly' to be warden of the scheme. In fact they appointed a young woman with a small daughter. Marjory Sinclair was interviewed three times, the third interview also involving her husband who had to be assessed for suitability. 'Would he be supportive to a warden who was on-call 24/7 and who would need to be getting out of bed at night?'

Marjory Sinclair, later a founding member of the National Wardens Association, was one of a long line of Viewpoint wardens, the first of whom had been appointed in 1957.[132] The first 'wardens' were intended to be 'just to be a person on hand.'[133] Often they were retired 'professional women' themselves, including a number of former missionaries. They received no salary – indeed the first appointee, at Deborah House, paid a small rent – but they benefited from free accommodation and the guarantee of a place in a Viewpoint house when they retired. Miss McMahon was one such, living as a caring presence at Dell Court in Colinton before retiring to Old Farm Court.

With the appointment of women such as Marjory Sinclair, the role of warden became more formalised. 'House Notes' for the Residential Club in Inverleith Terrace, dated 1974, explained that 'an experienced warden will be in charge of the establishment and will be on call in cases of sudden illness ... She is not expected to answer door bells or take messages. The Warden has many duties in the house and should not be disturbed unnecessarily, but will give friendly help and advice.'[134] The guarantee of accommodation on retirement was still an attraction for many women who applied for the role – which went 'against the grain of standard practice', says Norman Dunhill, but was undoubtedly a significant aspect of what was 'an incredibly successful recruitment' process headed up by Joan Stephenson. These were individuals who regularly gave more than a hundred per cent. 'We're talking about women who put their heart and soul into it', says Marjory. She speaks of life in this period as 'a juggling act', recalling, as a fairly typical instance, welcoming the management committee ('the great and the good') through the front door of her scheme while awaiting the undertakers' arrival at the back door to collect a recently deceased resident.

The wardens 'were absolutely marvellous', agrees Elisabeth Penman. 'They were paid a pittance and worked all the hours that God gave, organising things for tenants.' On occasions, this gave rise to a flexible interpretation of the rules. Norman Dunhill cites a warden at Lynedoch Place who was 'prepared to cope with a certain number of "extra-care" people, though this was not strictly what the residence was designed for. She kept people there longer than they would have been otherwise.' Her approach was not unique. To some extent, it was mirrored throughout the organisation (Viewpoint recruited wardens who wanted to do the job and were not just interested in terms and conditions, writes Susan Maclennan) and the ethos was modelled by Norman Dunhill and Miss Ingham's determination to do what they thought was right even when this conflicted with statutory requirements. There was a downside, though, to what might be regarded as a healthy response to rigid legality. A failure, on occasions, to ensure a consistency of approach throughout the organisation allowed some individuals, as we shall see in the next chapter, to assume a degree of autonomy that created headaches for the Viewpoint committees.

During the period that Gillespie Crescent was being constructed, another scheme was opened at St Alban's Road. It was located on the almost one-acre site of former playing fields belonging to George Watson's Ladies' College, which had recently amalgamated with the boys' school to form the modern-day co-educational George Watson's College. Susan Maclennan observes that this scheme fitted well with Viewpoint's aim of placing small-scale dwellings in the heart of residential areas, allowing older people to remain in the district where they were known and with which they were familiar. Such schemes, she notes, were not instantly recognisable as Sheltered Housing since Viewpoint wished them to blend in with the adjacent properties.

One other fact marks out the St Alban's Road scheme as a landmark project in the development of the Association. The mix of accommodation also included two-bedroom flats, allowing the possibility of couples sharing, and for the first time a male resident was housed in a Viewpoint development. (Men would also be housed at Gillespie Crescent. 'It was good to have men around', recalls Marjory Sinclair: 'the women behaved better!') In fact, regulations at the time laid down that a two-bedroom flat should accommodate three people, meaning that families were an option, but this was not an avenue that Viewpoint was keen to go down and once again no-one questioned Viewpoint's idiosyncratic decision.[135]

Meanwhile, another Sheltered Housing scheme, Old Farm Court in Colinton, had been acquired from Cluny Housing Association. Cluny had planned a spacious and imaginative development but found this impossible to carry through in the financial climate of the time, and offered the site to Viewpoint for development within the more restricted standards acceptable to the authorities. The location was a good one, close to the shopping centre of Colinton Village and existing on a site that had once been the home farm belonging to Old Colinton House. Under Viewpoint's management, the development eventually offered a large number of two, three and four-bedroom flats, mostly on the basis of Sheltered Accommodation. Nowadays, a stone trough at the main entrance to the scheme is one of the few indications that this was ever a working farm.

Over the nine years following the 1974 Housing Act, Viewpoint completed 13 Sheltered Housing schemes within Edinburgh, as well as two schemes outwith the city boundaries. On the eve of opening the Association's 500th sheltered house, in the 48-flat development at Cameron Crescent, Norman Dunhill spoke at length to

The Scotsman newspaper. 'Perhaps some of our earlier schemes were a bit big', he acknowledges. 'We've settled now to around 40–60 units to a scheme, although you really have to build to suit the site.'

> *Most of these schemes are fairly conventional Sheltered Housing developments, although the society have broken new ground with a few developments which combine standard sheltered accommodation with flatlets, the latter supported by communal dining facilities. The award-winning Lynedoch House is such a scheme, as is Inverard House in Arboretum Road.*[136]

Lynedoch, which stands proudly above Dean Bridge, had won its awards for the building's architecture. Like several other developments at this time, Lynedoch was designed to contrast boldly with the buildings around it rather than blend into the background. With what Norman Dunhill describes as 'a hard, professional team', Viewpoint produced a string of unique, imaginative and striking buildings that seem to reflect the confidence and forward momentum of Viewpoint in the late 1970s.

Some of these developments made a significant contribution to the changing appearance of Scotland's capital city. Lynedoch itself was designed by Roland Wedgwood Associates, the firm behind the rehabilitation of the distinctive mid-Victorian Rosemount Buildings in Fountainbridge. At Lynedoch, they built out from a former YWCA hostel with a 'pale brick expressionist block of flats'[137] that seems to rise in conjoined columns out of the old high stone wall below. The building featured a glazed, rooftop conservatory with fine views across the Forth Estuary towards Fife. For this work, they were awarded a Royal Institute of British Architects award and, the following year, Viewpoint received a Saltire Society award. The scheme was notable for the way it had been developed on a constricted corner site, and was of sufficient interest to attract visitors from overseas.

The flats that, according to *The Scotsman*, 'rejuvenated' the corner of West Richmond Street and Nicolson Street were unusual for another reason. This time, Viewpoint built above a row of shops, completing the build with a sixth-storey residents' lounge which, as at Lynedoch, was glazed in like a conservatory and offered 'some of the best views of the city'. Residents of Argyle Park House at number 10 Argyle Park Terrace might have disagreed. From their unique modern build of flats, with its unusually bulky roof, they also had access to a top floor common room that included a kitchen and gallery overlooking the leafy Meadows.

Perhaps the most distinctive of Viewpoint's properties opened during this period, however, is Nicholas Groves-Raines' Cameron Crescent, situated near the present-day Cameron Toll shopping centre and the location of that notable 500th sheltered unit. With its brown brick cladding, trimmed with cream brick edging, the building attracted comment from architects and passers-by alike, some disparaging it as 'London lavatorial'. It was the featured building in a special edition of the Scottish Architects' newspaper, *Prospect*, devoted to building in brick. ('It's still the best way of keeping the wolf from the door', ran the inside advertisement.) The paper described the mix of 28 one-person and 15 two-person sheltered flats, built on a restricted area that had been the site of Prestonfield Church. This, like Lynedoch, was a good example of Viewpoint's innovative use of gap sites within the city. At each end, it noted, the design was linked to existing buildings that were being refurbished as part of the project.[138] Twenty-five years on, the 'North County Victorian industrial' style of Cameron Crescent[139] remains a striking architectural presence in south Edinburgh, with a freshness of appearance that has eluded some more high-profile developments that were constructed with fashionable sandstone at the same time. There were those who questioned Viewpoint's policy of commissioning such high-profile, non-standard building projects. Surely they represented an extravagant use of public funds? Norman Dunhill is of the opinion that they didn't cost the tax-payer much more than lower spec projects, but that wasn't the view taken by decision-makers in the Housing Corporation – and their opinion, together with the perception of Viewpoint as a middle-class organisation, would have a bearing on Viewpoint's later difficulties in getting funding for further projects.

However, not all Viewpoint's buildings made such a strong impression or caused so many raised eyebrows. The Restalrig Road South development, completed in 1982, was ingeniously tucked into an old part of the historic village of Restalrig. Other schemes were developed along the familiar Viewpoint lines of extending or building around existing large houses, a number of them properties of interest in their own right. The main house at Lauder Road – part of an Extra-Sheltered development – originally belonged to the family of Stewart Clark, one of the founding brothers of the hugely successful 19th century cotton thread business based in Paisley (nowadays amalgamated within Coats plc).[140] Inverard House at Inverleith Gardens had been the home of members of the Salvesen family (of Christian Salvesen Ltd) and also the Duncan family, known as Edinburgh-based chocolate makers.

Before Viewpoint purchased Inverard in 1978, it had seen life as a maternity home and as a nursing home, but since the 1950s the house had served as a 'Home of Rest' run by the Aged Christian Friend Society of Scotland. The Society had been formed to provide pensions for poor (Protestant) Christian men and women aged over 60, and to create 'Cottage Houses' for special cases. A number of these were built in Colinton.[141] In the late 1970s, the Directors saw the prevailing trend in housing and the potential for building Sheltered Housing within the grounds of Inverard. However, it soon became clear that the costs for such a development were going to be too high for the Society to bear. It didn't qualify as a Housing Association and therefore wasn't eligible for the necessary loans for such an ambitious project. Viewpoint was approached and the property sold on the under-standing that Viewpoint would carry out the plans envisaged by the Society. A number of bungalows were duly constructed in the house gardens in 1980. For the third time in four years, the Association had completed more than one hundred Sheltered Housing units for the elderly – at Inverard House, Argyle Park Terrace and 204 Morningside Drive. In addition, the first occupants moved into Viewpoint's second scheme in Colinton, 'Woodthorpe'.[142] 'Indeed the building programme went rather better than anticipated and there are hopes of exceeding the hundred completions in 1981–82.'[143]

A glance at a street map of Edinburgh shows very quickly the geographical spread of properties that Viewpoint had achieved across the city by the early 1980s: from Inverard House in the north of the city to Cameron Crescent and Cameron Park on the Southside; from Restalrig, to the east of Arthur's Seat, across to the Colinton schemes in the foothills of the Pentlands. No longer was the Association constrained by the more limited ambition of housing single, professional women within easy distance of Princes Street. (In any case, the expansion of the public transport bus system by Lothian Regional Transport since 1975 had surely redefined what was considered 'easy.') More important was the hope of finding homes for older people within the areas with which they were familiar. Joan Stephenson confirms this strategy of buying up properties, Monopoly-style, across the board, noting the failed attempts to find suitable buildings or gap sites in the Corstorphine and, for a while, Blackhall areas of the city. 'Viewpoint Housing Association can hardly lay claim to being a large association, even by Scottish standards,' reported *The Scotsman*, 'but there can be few, if any, other such associations in the country which have built so many Sheltered Housing schemes in such a concentrated area.'[144]

At the same time, the Association was expanding into new areas – down the east coast to Prestonpans and across the Forth into Fife. Both Prestonpans and St Andrews saw the completion of developments in 1982–83. 'Preston Tower' was named for the 14th–15th century monument adjacent to the scheme. Indeed, Viewpoint entered into an agreement with the Local Authority to manage the green space (complete with a putting green) around the Tower.

At City Park in St Andrews, Viewpoint re-developed the former Gibson Hospital. A large villa had been built here in 1851 by a timber importer and philanthropist, William Gibson, described in his obituary as 'one of the City's distinguished native citizens.'[145] His Will bequeathed a sufficient sum of money for 'the erection and maintenance of a hospital for the benefit of the aged, sick and infirm people of the City and Parish of St Andrews', and following his death in 1862 the Trustees of his endowment agreed to build the Gibson Hospital in the extensive grounds of City Park. This was opened in 1884. Almost a hundred years later, Viewpoint's initial intention was to create holiday accommodation for residents[146] but, in the event, demand was such that the Association provided instead a development of Sheltered and Extra-Sheltered Housing in Gibson's house – characteristically adding a modern and contrasting wing onto the original building.

The demand for such accommodation reflected the national statistics. Older people were living longer. To Marjorie Sinclair, the reasons were obvious: 'It's not rocket science! Keep people warm and they need fewer clothes. If they need fewer clothes, they are less restricted and fall less. They feel better because they have more mobility. They live longer as a result.' And with longevity comes, on the one hand, a desire for continued independence while that is possible, and on the other hand, the requirement for different degrees of supported living as time goes by. Norman Dunhill's greatest horror, he would say, was of seeing (and more to the point, having to provide for) three generations of older people: in their sixties, their eighties and their hundreds. But that's precisely what was happening. In the 1981 census, 17 per cent of the Scottish population (846,000 people) were over retirement age, and in the over-75 category, women outnumbered men two to one.[147]

Joan Stephenson saw the changing demographic in the numbers of aging residents. It was at City Park that Viewpoint's first 100th birthday was celebrated. The Provost and a piper were present, and an iced sponge cake had been made in the shape of the resident's own house. Perhaps because she liked the cake so much, she refused to cut it – 'so it was wine and biscuits instead'. At Inverleith Terrace, the hundred candles lit for another centenarian had the effect of setting off the fire alarm, resulting in a contingent of yellow-uniformed firemen joining in the celebration.

The pressure for new properties and for more intense degrees of care was not easing up, but how Viewpoint was to finance its planned endeavours was a source of growing concern. A few new developments were underway but undeniably Viewpoint's building programme was slowing down. Three years earlier, Norman had already reported that, 'in common with most Housing Associations, Viewpoint ended the year with unexpected problems and a feeling of frustration.' This frustration, he continues:

> ... *was a direct result of the [Conservative] Government's restrictions on the resources to be made available to the Housing Corporation and Local Authorities for lending to*

> *Housing Associations. The cash available, although increasing, is not sufficient to match the approved programme which appears to have been halved. Schemes which should have gone out to tender in 1981–82 are being held back and the purchase of new sites is virtually impossible.*[148]

Norman Dunhill's anger is palpable, and it's a mood that grows with successive annual reports:

> *The Association ended the year with hopes that the construction of at least two of the three remaining delayed schemes would be able to start in 1982–83, but it is disappointing to record that no entirely new projects were approved ... The main frustration for the Association's staff remains the task of turning away so many needy applicants.* [149]

And:

> *... for the second year running no new projects were approved.*[150]

Ian Penman puts it simply. 'There were very obvious Tory cuts in public expenditure on housing, but the commitments of Housing Associations remained at the same level.' In that interview given to *The Scotsman* in May of 1983, Norman Dunhill was given an opportunity to describe in no uncertain terms the situation as he now saw it.

> *'Two years ago we had a substantial ongoing programme of building,' says Mr Dunhill. 'But the cutbacks in public*

spending effectively slowed that down. The Salisbury Road scheme that we started this week should really have been started two years ago ... This isn't a shortage of opportunities; it's a shortage of money' ... The association have a 'colossal' waiting list, he adds ... in the region of 3,000 including enquiries, and while much of that will be duplicated on other housing agencies' lists, it indicates the level of need there is in this area. 'Edinburgh has left its main Sheltered Housing provision to housing associations like ourselves, and while our 500 houses have helped, we still haven't been able to solve the problem.'

'It's not the [Viewpoint] society as such that suffers from the cut backs but the old people themselves who are unable to get sheltered accommodation, and time is not on their side ... '[151]

Chapter 11
Where there's a will …

The second half of the 1980s was a period of mixed fortunes for Viewpoint, as for many Housing Associations. With Mrs Thatcher's squeeze on public funds at its tightest, the Annual Reports from this period describe an organisation locked in to a kind of 'holding pattern'. Consolidation, upgrading, a policy of 'progressive improvement' and modernisation are the words that colour descriptions of Viewpoint's activity most strongly. There is a clear sense that the organisation is feeling held back. Momentum has been lost and such growth as there is within the organisation is failing to match the relatively rapid expansion of the first half of Norman Dunhill's tenure as Director. When Bob Duff took over that role in 1992, he considered Viewpoint close to being 'moribund'. Other, rather newer Housing Associations had already succeeded in building more housing units than Viewpoint. Bob perceived a lack of forward planning and, critically, a reluctance on the part of Scottish funding bodies to prioritise Viewpoint as a supplier of specialist housing for older people.

Undoubtedly, the downturn in Viewpoint's fortunes from 1985 onwards presents a gloomy picture – one that Norman Dunhill himself had forecast in his 1983 *Scotsman* interview. And yet there is another side to the story. Viewpoint had never been a one-trick pony and this period in particular is notable for the Association's attempts to diversify, both in the types of housing it offered and in how it went about financing it. Under Norman Dunhill's leadership, Viewpoint exhibited considerable imagination and a characteristic ability to take advantage of changing funding and legislative opportunities, such that the work undertaken in the late 1980s can be said to have shaped fundamentally the multi-faceted organisation that exists today.

As Viewpoint approached the mid-1980s, notwith-standing the difficult economic situation within which they were operating, Norman and the ever-determined Miss Ingham ensured that Viewpoint continued to aim high – though they were not always able to achieve all that they wanted. Often, their frustrations resulted from the mismatch between their aspirations for the older people they housed and the level at which the Local Authorities were prepared to approve government funding. At St Alban's, for example, Viewpoint wished to install central heating, which was expensive to install but cheaper to run for the residents themselves. Local government would fund only a cheaper electrical heating system. At the award-winning Lynedoch conversion and new build, Viewpoint wished to provide private toilets for each resident, whereas the statutory obligation at the time was to provide one toilet for every three residents. Nowadays, a private bathroom and toilet would be regarded as a given in order to ensure personal privacy and dignity, but because Viewpoint was exceeding government standards, the authorities wouldn't agree to pay for the additional facilities. Viewpoint had, therefore, to find the extra funding itself.

As already seen, fund raising lay at the heart of Viewpoint's social life and sense of 'family', with money from legacies and donations adding to what was possible by way of raising standards and adding 'extras'. During this period, also, some of the Association's older, non-sheltered flats were being sold off, among them some of the 'alphabet houses'. These properties were no longer considered suitable for modern Sheltered Accommodation. They were difficult to upgrade to the required standards and, in any case, the basement and upper floors were becoming even less attractive to prospective tenants than they had been previously. As tenants became older, their preference was more usually for ground floor accommodation. Joan Marshall recalls clearing the remaining furniture and fitments from Bridget and Hester Houses. No professional movers were hired – this was a family affair. She and Helen Ford, wages clerk with Viewpoint Benevolent, together with their husbands, did the job between them. Helen's husband, a builder by trade, provided an open van suitable for the purpose. (It also came in handy for Viewpoint's grand fund raising efforts in the Assembly Rooms, together with the van belonging to the Viewpoint painter.)

Raising funds from the sale of older properties, Norman used to say, meant that Viewpoint could at least put doors in some of the new properties, even if it couldn't prevent the slow-down in Viewpoint's building programme. Nevertheless some new projects were being completed during this period. Among them were flats in Blackhall, where Viewpoint had finally found a building opportunity on the site of the former Craigleith Quarry. The development at Maidencraig Crescent was named

Cockburn Court after the founder committee member (and later Chairman) of Viewpoint, Elizabeth Cockburn. Its design, with a geometric-shaped frontage and five-storey rise, has a loose family resemblance to the design of Lynedoch and was noted, at the time, for the depth of the foundations it required before building could commence.

In 1984, the first tenants also moved into St Stephen Place, Stockbridge. This project would prove to be the source of a long-running saga, as Viewpoint struggled to develop its proposed second phase, the creation of a further development of Extra-Sheltered Housing on the same site. Jack Fleming reported in 1986[152] that such a scheme was under consideration by the Housing Corporation, but the following year he writes that the funds that the Corporation were prepared to assign to the project were not enough to produce an economic scheme. As late as 1994, Jack's successor, Ian Penman, had to report continued delays to 'the development of 38 units of very Sheltered Housing on site at St Stephen Place'. The problem now was the difficulty of acquiring an adjacent parcel of land which would make the site viable, but he adds that 'hopefully, with the support of Edinburgh District Council which is seeking to acquire the land through a Compulsory Purchase Order, I will have better news to report next year.'[153] With some reluctance, the Council did finally proceed with the compulsory purchase. However, only in 1997 does the Annual Report include 20 units of Extra-Sheltered Housing at St Stephen Place among its list of new developments, at an estimated cost of £1.9 million.

Despite the progression of Cockburn Court and St

Stephen Place, something has gone wrong with Viewpoint's plans. It simply isn't developing at the rate that one might have expected. The tougher economic climate had something to do with this, but behind the scenes there lies another issue – a marked cooling of relations between Viewpoint and the Housing Corporation. It was a state of affairs that went back to 1981. The Government Treasury, to which the London-based Housing Corporation was answerable, had recently instituted a new system for controlling expenditure. It allowed far less flexibility than previously for extenuating circumstances and negotiation at the end of any financial year. In January 1981, pressure was placed on the Housing Corporation to take action in order to avoid a projected overspend for that financial year. A memo was duly circulated stating that, as of the date of the memo, no Housing Association should enter any new contract until the end of March that year. And no Housing Association did – except Viewpoint. The memo had arrived on Norman Dunhill's desk on the very day that he received a favourably priced contract in response to Viewpoint's tender for a development at Haugh Park. It was, he argued, in the best interests of Viewpoint to accept it.

The Housing Corporation reacted angrily. Resignations were called for. None were forthcoming but Viewpoint had now made a name for itself that it wouldn't shake off completely for some years to come. The Corporation (which shortly afterwards devolved more power to Scotland) already had concerns about Viewpoint's expenditure on what were seen as unnecessarily elaborate and self-regarding architectural projects.

There was also some question about whether Viewpoint was catering for the most needy categories of society. Now the Corporation was making difficult enquiries about the extent of the Director's ability to act without reference to his Board. Norman Dunhill and others countered by questioning the extent to which the Housing Corporation supervised and monitored the affairs of individual Housing Associations.

Early Minutes of the Viewpoint Housing Executive Sub-Committee, formed in the wake of the incident, offer evidence of the constraints that the organisation now felt itself working under. Barely a single idea could be mooted without the Housing Corporation say-so, yet the Corporation itself didn't move with any great alacrity. The Sheltered Housing development at Haugh Park suffered delays as a result, and the Committee was nervous of making any proposal that might receive a negative response.[154] It wouldn't be until after the arrival of a new Director ten years later that an easier working relationship would be achieved. In the meantime, persuading the Corporation that Viewpoint would be a good steward of its money was easier said than done, and Norman Dunhill's job was made rather more difficult than it had been.

Jack Fleming, who helped to resolve the initial row, remembers Norman as a 'very vigorous and an efficient organiser', but not someone who operated in the mould of most civil servants. He was, says one former employee, 'the visionary' who got things done. Aside from his work for Viewpoint, for example, Norman was a driving force behind the restoration of Robert Owen's 18th cotton mill village in New Lanark (now a World Heritage Site with its own Housing Association), for which he received an MBE. Passionate about the need for social housing and adamant that high standards be adhered to, he reacted against what he perceived to be unnecessary regulation, and resented what he regarded as the dilution of Viewpoint's ability to offer the best deal for its tenants. This, as Norman himself was well aware, made him unpopular with a lot of people – though in retrospect it is not something that he is sorry about. He was doing, as others attest with some admiration, what he believed in. 'Why do we need to do this?' he would cry, says Joan Stephenson, 'and then he would just bash on.' Not that he was alone – this was, in many respects, 'the Viewpoint way'. Joan herself recalls feeling that too much consultation only caused more difficulty. In her pragmatic way, she instances the admittedly more domestic need to decide where a rotary dryer was to be placed on a shared lawn. 'There were six couples in the residence, so I would get six different views about where it should go.'

Perhaps providing a useful counter-balance to Norman's style, Joan Stephenson recalls Miss Ingham endeavouring at this time to maintain good relations with the Housing Corporation. 'She was old and set in her ways,' says Joan, who had known her for 12 years, 'but she knew the right people. She worked hard to get her way with the Housing Corporation, and even with Norman in post was involved in setting policy – though she drove him mad.' Above all, she concludes, Miss Ingham kept to her ideals. In her honour, Viewpoint named its new Salisbury Road property Ingham Court. It opened to residents in 1985. This typical Edinburgh detached villa, used to house Viewpoint's ground staff until development money was made available, had been a Jewish school ('Shul') and was sold to Viewpoint by the Edinburgh Jewish community, whose synagogue still stands opposite. 'I would ... like to thank you on my own behalf,' Miss Ingham wrote to Marjory Sinclair, who had been installed as warden following her time at Gillespie Crescent, '– because I know that the idea sprang from you, of calling this house after me. As you can guess, I have always found my name a nuisance, but I am particularly pleased to be associated with this venture. Indeed I am thrilled.' She continues in more general terms, describing the context within which Viewpoint was now operating:

> *It is sad that Government finance has dried up, and the developers who seem to have so much money available are taking our Sheltered Housing. Unfortunately of course, they are also able to find sites. I am just going to Gullane to look at a site for the [Viewpoint] Benevolent, but I am told that there is no chance of getting it, as the developers can offer far more than we can. But where does that leave those who have no capital and can only afford to rent? Precisely no-where. It does make one wonder about Brazen images!*[155]

It was as Miss Ingham described. Following the opening of Ingham Court, Viewpoint had no new houses under construction for the first time in ten years. The 1986 'Review of the Year' offers a concise summary of the situation. It highlights the standstill in construction and the need to pursue private sector funding, and Jack Fleming reiterates Norman Dunhill's frustration that it is those on the Viewpoint Sheltered Housing waiting list (now over five thousand) who are being deprived by the reduction in public funding. Then he turns to the matter of the ever increasing age of the Association's tenants and the consequent demand to give special attention to the needs of the frail elderly:

> *Unfortunately, although other Associations recognise Viewpoint's considerable experience in this field and come to us for advice, the funding agencies have been slow to encourage new experiments in this area. The need for extra care housing for the elderly is increasing daily and the Association is convinced that there could be great advantage and increased economy in adding extra care to more conventional Sheltered Housing and so providing a comprehensive care service for the elderly.*[156]

Here again, the Association is articulating its desire to establish a 'hierarchy of care', and, for the first time, the report notes the establishment of a relationship with St Raphael's Housing Association, which has been able to meet the needs of some who require Nursing Home care – 'though the reduction in the DHSS board and lodging allowances, which still do not meet existing costs, means that this assistance is not available to all our tenants.'[157]

The majority of extra care undertaken by Viewpoint was being managed by Viewpoint Benevolent, which owned the Homes at Lennox Row and Ettrick Road.[158] In 1987, Viewpoint bought the small house at 14a Ettrick Road adjacent to the existing schemes at numbers 12 and 14 with a view to improving the provision of accommodation for the frail elderly. But private funding was going to have to be sought if any significant developments were going to be made. Meanwhile, notes and letters relating to a number of the Benevolent schemes suggest that, not for the first time, staffing matters were a cause of constant headaches for Miss Ingham and the Viewpoint Benevolent Committee. At times these notes also make clear that the attitudes of Miss Ingham and her colleagues had been formulated in a relatively narrow world. One such note, headed 'Trouble at Drummond', reads:

> *Mrs M has applied for the post of Assistant Warden. She is said to be quite 'rough' but reliable. She was an auxiliary nurse in the Simpson Memorial Hospital for 13 years. Miss P the Warden has elected to do the meals and she is said to be 'a good plain cook'. Nevertheless most of the meals are prepared by an 18 year old from a housing scheme.[159] The 'schoolgirls' who help with the evening meal are quite out of hand (one of them sings in a band and is more interested in the band than her job).*

At Ettrick Road, meanwhile, the matron was causing Miss Ingham some concern:

> *She is* not *a registered Nurse [and] consequently it has been impossible to get a Nurse as depute Matron ... The real trouble seems to be that while she is capable and cares for the residents, she tends to 'run the place without any regard to anyone else.'*

Partly, Miss Ingham was concerned about Matron's style. 'I think she put a high emphasis on speech,' observes Joan Marshall, 'and certainly did not like people that spoke loudly or harshly, which could be referred to as "rough".'

Moira Shearer, star of *The Red Shoes*, attends a Viewpoint fund raiser. Edward French hovers in the background

Edward French and helpers in the bric-a-brac shop at the '100 Club'

An Easter Market in Edinburgh's Assembly Rooms

Pamela Williamson, Joan Marshall and Fiona Verth prepare to play 100 holes of golf in aid of the £1 Million Target Fund

A summer fair in the grounds of George Heriot's School

'London lavatorial'? The distinctive brickwork of Balfour House, Cameron Crescent

The award-winning extension of Lynedoch House, overlooking Dean Bridge

The Duke of Edinburgh meets his new neighbours at the opening of Croft-an-Righ. Norman Dunhill on the right; Jack Fleming with back to camera

World War One veterans outside St Raphael's Hospital in the Grange area of Edinburgh

Peggy Home and staff of the Stockbridge budget shop handover a cheque to the Sisters at St. Raphael's. George Home, back; Norman Dunhill, right

Norma Major at the opening of the converted St Raphael's Residential Home

Staff training increased in the 1990s under the leadership of Bob Duff

Dan Orr and Meg McNeill share a joint 100th birthday celebration at Inverard

Above. With its distinctive mix of housing and care, Viewpoint continues to welcome new tenants

Left. A new rose is chosen by Cockburn Court resident June Grainger to mark Viewpoint's 60th anniversary. She has given it the name 'New Life'

The Ettrick Road matron could come across in that slightly bossy way. But – as Miss Ingham was also well aware – she was at heart a caring person. Miss Ingham's main concern was that the matron's desire to care could lead, on some occasions, to awkward unilateral decisions. As Norman Dunhill was aware, the Ettrick Road appointee wasn't the first warden or matron to keep a resident within her care even when that care exceeded the remit of the Home. A letter is sent from Miss Ingham on September 30, 1987:

> *Your own duties are* primarily *concerned with the welfare of Residents. The health and mental capacity of the Residents. It has to be remembered that these are ladies of considerable experience of the world. Consequently they have to be encouraged to* enjoy the same standard that they have had in the past. *I am aware that you still have Miss M with you,* but *she is now requiring care in a medical ward. This is classified as a Residential Home. It is* not *a Nursing Home, and as I have told you before, while the Committee is grateful for what you do to keep the older ladies with their sense of security, it is not up to you to change the character of the house. The other residents have rights as well as those who are now past our type of care.*

'Our type of care' ... Recognition, once again, that Viewpoint is unable to offer yet the full continuity of care through older age to which it undoubtedly aspires.

Shortly after writing that letter in 1987, Miss Ingham retired from her role as Secretary and Manager of Viewpoint Benevolent. After forty years of deeply committed service on the organisation's behalf, she took up residence in Viewpoint's own Lennox Row.

Another change at Viewpoint, related to Miss Ingham's retirement, was the reorganisation its structure. Viewpoint Association took over direct management of the properties at Drummond Place and Inverleith Terrace with a view to carrying out modifications previously planned by Viewpoint Benevolent. In addition, a decision was made to establish the Viewpoint Trust. The Trust had no responsibility for managing property but did take on the administration of the charitable funds raised over the years by 'Benevolent', and was charged with administering effectively any further donations and bequests made to the Association. As previously, this left Viewpoint Housing Association itself to concentrate on managing and maintaining the bulk of the organisation's housing stock. It did so, argues Susan Maclennan, with 'the best qualified housing management department for its size in Scotland'. Among the tasks it undertook was to upgrade Miss Ingham's original purpose-built flats in the Grange Loan area, and the properties at Cameron Park and Melgund Terrace which, by modern standards, now appeared small and old-fashioned. It was now, also, that Viewpoint again diversified its work in order to respond to changing needs and challenges.

Susan Maclennan observes that the original Viewpoint Society had started out by raising private funds and loans; as time progressed, the re-named Association was then able to take advantage of public funding. But now, the changing economic climate, the re-organisation of housing funding in Scotland and Viewpoint's cool relations with the Housing

Corporation, forced Norman Dunhill to consider once again private funding sources. Out of necessity, however, emerged another pioneering concept: co-ownership Sheltered Housing.

> *It occurred to me that co-ownership would be a suitable way to create affordable accommodation for elderly people who wished to retain ownership of their home but found that the investment in traditional private Sheltered Housing was too high for them.*[160]

What Norman had in mind was an arrangement whereby the tenants of a Sheltered Housing scheme would also be its owners. This could be achieved if every tenant was also a member of a new Association formed especially to oversee the new development. The formation of a new tenant-led Association would allow the scheme to qualify for tax relief on a private loan, which Viewpoint would take out to build it in the first place. Once it was built, Viewpoint would manage – not own – the scheme on a day-to-day basis on behalf of the new Association.

Viewpoint spent six years negotiating these arrangements and the result was the Croft-an-Righ Housing Association Ltd., the first co-ownership Sheltered Housing scheme in Scotland. Begun in May 1987, the £4 million scheme comprised 96 one and two-bedroom sheltered flats in Edinburgh, priced initially at £38,000 and £48,000. The building was funded by a loan from the Nationwide Anglia Building Society. It created considerable publicity for Viewpoint, not so much because of its novel management arrangements as for the fact that the chosen site for the scheme was the former St Ann's Brewery in Abbeyhill, directly adjacent to Holyrood Palace. This proximity, observed Norman dryly, meant that 'an extra planning exercise had to be gone through' – adding:

> *'We would hope that the Queen will be very pleased with the new development because it will be a great improvement on the eyesore that is there now. The site shares a very large boundary with the Palace.'*[161]

The horse-shoe arrangement of flats sits close to a 16th century house, from which the scheme takes its name, meaning 'Field of the King'. Once accessed from Holyrood through the Abbey's burial ground, the original house is described variously as having been built for the Regent Moray in 1588 and having been gifted by James VI to his favourite servant, 'French'.

The Press loved the story of the Queen's new next-door neighbours and when the Duke of Edinburgh came for the formal opening ceremony in June 1988, one paper ran a story headed, 'Dorothy's right royal cup of tea.'

> *Pensioner Dorothy Webster is looking forward to meeting her next-door neighbour for the first time ... for he's none other than Prince Philip ... 'I'll offer him tea and biscuits, but I've nothing stronger in the house,' said Dorothy yesterday. She added: 'Neighbours should be friendly, shouldn't they?'*[162]

In a document describing the funding and management arrangements, Viewpoint listed the advantages of co-ownership housing. They included the provision of communal facilities such as laundries, guest rooms and gardening maintenance 'on a less costly basis than if met on an individual basis'. A range of carefully thought through benefits was used to attract prospective tenants to the scheme – its prestigious and convenient location, of course, but also weekly visits by a fishmonger and the availability of a stamp machine, post box and 'same day' prescription service. There was, too, the welcome freedom from responsibility in dealing with repairs.

> *Experience is that elderly people do not wish to have the problem[s] which ownership tends to bring but at the same time do not wish to lose the independence which ownership gives. Taken overall, co-ownership provides an arrangement which meets both of these wishes.*[163]

For Viewpoint itself there was the additional benefit of 'tax concessions available to the Association on the loan repayments which would not be available to an ordinary tenant.'

The loan from Nationwide Anglia represented, as the newspapers noted, the first time that a development of this kind had been totally privately funded. In this respect the arrangements can be said to have pre-empted provisions within the 1988 Housing Act. This legislation meant that private borrowing to fund development became the norm – with a consequence that Associations were increasingly exposed to an environment of risk.[164] The other significant piece in the jigsaw of arrangements that allowed Viewpoint to pursue the privately-funded co-ownership arrangement was the use of loan stock – the style of funding that had last featured in Viewpoint's records as a concept used to help set up Miss Cunningham's Four Freedoms Housing Society, though probably in a different form. The loan stock funding solution was, says Henry McIntosh, 'a concept of its time' and a response to prevailing tax legislation. Viewpoint was to employ it most extensively for Croft-an-Righ and again for the formation of another of small Housing Association, Kilravock.

Loan stock offered charitable Housing Associations a way of securing development finance to build houses. A building society would provide a development mortgage but this was required to be paid off once the building was complete – and the money wasn't going to come from sales of the property, which were built only for rent. To do this, each property was allocated a cost – not a valuation but, rather, a percentage of the original Building Society loan based on the number of individual units within the scheme. Each new resident would then loan the Association part of their property cost up front on moving in – effectively, a substantial down-payment on the rent they would have to pay monthly. The more capital they put in the first place, the lower the monthly rent. In the case of Croft-an-Righ, tenants were required to pay at least 50 per cent of the property cost. The unique feature of loan stock was that these down-payments were repayable to the resident or resident's estate on their departure or death, and then the payment would be re-made by the successor tenant. In this way, the Building Society was always guaranteed, by way of a loan stock promissory note, that its loan would be repaid.

In the case of Kilravock, in Edinburgh's desirable

Grange area, the initial building costs were in the region of £6 million and each property was allocated a loan stock 'cost' of between £30,000 and £50,000. Clearly, neither Croft-an-Righ nor Kilravock could be classed as traditional social housing given their requirement that a tenant had sufficient capital to be paid as loan stock. Indeed, the schemes could appear elitist, admits Viewpoint's former Director of Central Services, Henry McIntosh. 'A few very wealthy people did take advantage of the [Kilravock] scheme because the area suited them.' (In fact, Viewpoint had some difficulty in filling the final loan stock flats through its own waiting lists and was forced, for the first time, to advertise its property on the open market. With its well designed flats in one of Edinburgh's most sought-after residential districts, Kilravock was, read the advertising particulars, 'undoubtedly one of Edinburgh's most prestigious private Sheltered Housing developments.')

However, says Henry, both Croft-an-Righ and Kilravock provided an option for people who were excluded from traditional social housing precisely because they had too much capital or income to be considered but too little to be able to afford other appropriate accommodation. 'The vast majority [of prospective residents] were trapped by the very level of savings they had and this scheme served their needs.' Often, such older people required a limited level of care and oversight, despite not meeting the financial criteria set for more usual forms of social housing. Croft-an-Righ and Kilravock 'gave them community and an element of care that was very much in line with the early intentions of Viewpoint.'[165]

Kilravock, like Croft-an-Righ, was established as a separate Housing Association. It represented one of a growing number of housing partnerships. While Viewpoint provided management services to the two co-ownership schemes, it also managed two other housing complexes, Isaac Mackie (in Elie, Fife) and Lennox Tower (in Balerno). Where Kilravock differed from these schemes was in its relationship to a far broader development – in size and scope, Viewpoint's most ambitious to date. The Kilravock co-ownership apartments were just one facet of a development that had grown out of Viewpoint's increasingly close relationship with the adjacent St Raphael's Hospital in the Grange area of Edinburgh.

St Raphael's was already a well-established Edinburgh institution by the time Miss Cunningham founded Viewpoint. After the end of the First World War, the hospital had been set up in a large, turreted house located in extensive grounds bounded by Oswald Road, South Oswald Road and Blackford Avenue. The building itself had originally been named Kilravock House. It was built by Hugh Rose Jr., eldest son of Hugh Rose who had founded the 'Craig and Rose' paint company, known as manufacturers of the original Forth Rail Bridge paint. He named the house after Kilravock Castle in Invernessshire, the seat of Clan Rose since 1460 – an association that would eventually be revived in the choice of name for Kilravock Housing Association, established on the land adjacent to the original villa.

In 1919, Kilravock House was acquired by the Scottish branch of the Red Cross and the Ministry of Pensions as a Home for severely disabled servicemen. At the instigation of Lady Anne Kerr, sister of the Duke of Norfolk and married into the Lothian family, the Sisters of the Little Company of Mary were invited to run the Home. The Little Company of Mary, known also as 'The Blue Nuns', was an international sisterhood that over the years established major hospitals in Sydney, Australia, in South Africa and in South America.

At first, only victims of the Great War were admitted to the hospital – the first being described in the hospital journal as a 'paralysed and incurable Protestant'. The last remaining veteran would live there until he died in 1958. Over the years, changes were made. The Little Company of Mary acquired the hospital from the Red Cross, renaming it St Raphael's after the biblical archangel (whose name means 'God has healed') and building St David's Ward in memory of Lady Anne's son, who had been killed during the war. In 1929, the hospital's first female ward was opened. The Sisters provided all the staffing for St Raphael's, including its surgeons, and as the number of war victims reduced, it became used more and more as a hospital and nursing home for civilians. Susan Maclennan recalls that generations of older Edinburgh citizens knew St Raphael's as the place to go to for teeth and appendix treatments, though in fact the fully-equipped operating theatre had the capacity to undertake a far wider range of surgical procedures.

In 1948, the hospital opted to remain outwith the National Health Service. As the building was extended to meet the needs of local elderly people and general patients it remained the only Catholic hospital in the East of Scotland. It was here, in 1972, that George Home's wife, Peggy, underwent a serious operation. The care and friendship she received from the Sisters led to the couple's close friendship with them over the next three decades and to Peggy's work at the Stockbridge charity shop. So much needed doing in the building, they realised. The windows were very drafty, George recalls, and the facilities were badly in need of replacement. As a 16-year-old recruit to the Royal Bank of Scotland, he had worked in the small Blackford branch just along the road from St Raphael's and he remembered the Sisters at that time coming in to do business. Now a senior executive within the organisation, he used his contacts to form a small committee and organise an appeal to renew the windows and upgrade other facilities.

However, escalating costs meant that St Raphael's was becoming increasingly difficult to run. The Sisters were getting older and new members of staff were difficult to come by. Moreover, their living quarters were in need of renovation. The new private Murrayfield Hospital was being opened on the other side of the city, in Corstorphine and St Raphael's found itself the object of a possible takeover arrangement. Norman Dunhill refers to a possible Murrayfield takeover; George Home speaks of American interest. But with no en suite facilities, St Raphael's presented difficulties for any prospective buyer and, in any case, it seems that the Sisters had reservations about any such takeover scheme.

In 1982 the Little Company of Mary decided to discontinue the use of the nursing home buildings for surgical and medical care. Norman Dunhill was brought in as an advisor and the decision was made to form the St Raphael's Housing Association and convert the hospital, with the help of Viewpoint, into a nursing home for the long term care of the frail elderly. Between October 1984 and January 1986, the existing hospital wards and operating theatres were converted into 37 single rooms and related facilities. The old X-Ray Department was converted into a small dining room and the main passenger lift was fitted with automatic doors. The total cost amounted to over £300,000.[166]

In 1989, Norman Dunhill wrote in the industry magazine, *Building*:

> *It was always the intention of the new St Raphael's Housing Association to provide a comprehensive care service for the elderly on the site. It was felt that this could best be done by marrying a Sheltered Housing development with the new nursing home facility. By adding some Extra-Sheltered accommodation to more conventional Sheltered Housing, it should be possible to offer a comprehensive care service; residents in the Sheltered Housing can be offered additional services from the nursing home as and when required, and they will be given priority if a move to a nursing home is unavoidable. It should be possible therefore for residents to remain on the site until they die if they so wish ...*
>
> *To enable the new Sheltered Housing to be built on a co-ownership basis, the Kilravock Housing Association was formed to complete the development ... it has also been possible to provide accommodation on the site for the Sisters of the Little Company of Mary, many of whom are now quite old. The Sisters previously lived in the old house, which is to become Viewpoint's main office.[167]*

A further £300,000 was estimated for the second stage of

the alterations and St Raphael's still had to raise over £245,000 to pay for the work already completed. Scottish businessman and philanthropist, Tom Farmer (himself a committed Catholic), was approached for assistance. He provided an accountant, recalls Norman, to assess the viability of Viewpoint's plans. His conclusion was that such an ambitious project was not financially viable. 'If we'd assessed all Viewpoint's developments on that basis,' comments Norman Dunhill, 'we'd have done very little. In this case, Mother Superior took the view that if you want to do something you find ways and means – which chimed very much with Viewpoint's philosophy.' The means came unexpectedly, in the shape of a £1.5 million gift, left to Viewpoint by a lady who, says Norman, 'liked what we did'. She is described as the last survivor of three spinster sisters, says George Home. The family had made its money in shipping, but little more was known about the reasons for making this gift.[168] It was the largest gift in the history of Viewpoint, and it provided much of the funding for the St Raphael's redevelopment.

The effect of the St Raphael's-Kilravock venture was, as Norman Dunhill envisaged, to widen the services available to Viewpoint tenants to include full nursing care. Norman recalls one instance of a couple in which the wife moved to St Raphael's for more sustained care, while the husband was able to stay in their home at Kilravock. It was, says Susan Maclennan, another pioneering step, and it tied in with the change of registration status by now accorded to Lennox Row and Inverleith Terrace. In 1988, with the support of the now well-established Viewpoint Trust, Viewpoint Housing Association funded an extension of the lift in Inverleith

Terrace to the top floor, thus making further rooms available to those who found the stairs difficult. At the same time, Inverleith was registered with the Lothian Regional Social Work Department, meaning that a higher level of care could be provided and that those tenants who needed financial assistance could obtain a higher rate of allowance from the Department of Social Security. Four years later, in a comparable move, Lennox House was extended and refurbished at a cost of £1 million, financed entirely by charitable giving. A re-opening ceremony was held in May 1992 and Lennox House registered with the Health Board.

Meanwhile, on April 1, 1991, a 'transfer of engage-ments' took place from St Raphael's Housing Association to Viewpoint. Seven years after work at St Raphael's had begun, and with the new care facilities in place, Norman Dunhill saw an opportunity of drawing together in a more coherent way the caring expertise that Viewpoint and St Raphael's had developed over the course of their respective histories. At the same time, a 'transfer of engagements' also took place from Viewpoint Benevolent Housing Association to Viewpoint Housing Association, thus consolidating the full range of Viewpoint's opera-tions within the single all-embracing organisation that Viewpoint is today.

Back in 1960, Miss Ingham had had great cause to worry about a Miss G, then resident at the Ettrick Road Home. She was requiring more care and attention than Viewpoint could give her and had no choice but 'to send a notice to Miss G's lawyer saying she must be evicted.'[169] Over the years, Viewpoint's hope was to prevent such a situation occurring again. The St Raphael's-Kilravock initiative was both a practical and symbolic embodiment of that hope being made a reality.

The new building at St Raphael's Nursing Home was opened formally on September 11, 1992 by Norma Major, wife of the then Prime Minister. 'My dear', commented one resident, 'you're much too old to wear a skirt that short!' St Raphael's now included an extension to the west of the main building, complete with en suite facilities, largely financed by a generous donation from The Tudor Trust, a charitable trust with the stated aim of working with people and organisations intent on achieving lasting change in their communities. At the same time, Mrs Major opened the new Viewpoint offices, relocated from 63 Northumberland Street to the original, turreted Kilravock House – now renamed Viewpoint House. The move from Northumberland Street had been underway ever since Norman Dunhill took Joan Marshall, now his PA, and Helen Ford to view St Raphael's and told them that they were to be 'the advance party'. Space at Northumberland Street was tight. Viewpoint Benevolent, which for a time had been located next door but one, had moved into number 63 with the Association, which made for cosy quarters. And so, for the next two years, Joan and Helen lived among the builders, together with their fund raising equipment, stands, banners, and a 'portable' computer that 'weighed a ton'.

Nowadays, the whole site comprises St Raphael's 47 Nursing Home places, Kilravock's 62 Sheltered Housing flats, and a busy, modern office. (Additionally, Marian House, formerly a residence for retired Sisters of the Little Company of Mary, was converted into an additional residential Care Home in the year 2000.) The whole development was a considerable achievement, and the final legacy of Norman Dunhill who retired shortly afterwards. He was, wrote Ian Penman at the time, 'a doughty and kenspeckle standard bearer right up to the time of his retirement.'[170]

The Association had developed considerably over the 18 years of his involvement. He had pursued Viewpoint's Sheltered Housing programme with vigour and under his tenure the Association had achieved the broad mix of housing and care to which it had aspired for so long. The redevelopment of St Raphael's was the culmination of that evolutionary process. Viewpoint had grown through partnership with smaller associations, some that it had established itself and some that it hadn't. It had also grown as a result of private financial investment, responding to the changing economic climate. These were patterns that, once established, have continued into the new millennium. Above all, 'we had a large group of "satisfied customers", Norman concludes, 'and not a lot of complaints.'

Viewpoint had been transformed and would hold on to the legacy of this period. However, it was also inevitable that the organisation should now move forward in new ways under new leadership. Norman remained on the Board of the Viewpoint Trust for another three years but opted, finally, to step back and watch Viewpoint's development from the wings.

In other ways, too, 1992 represented the end of an era. Number 63 Northumberland Street was finally sold at the end of the year, with its basement 'Petticoat Lane' and its memories of Norman Dunhill doing battle with red tape and of Miss Ingham placing sweeties on her assistants' desks. The Tanfield budget shop had closed, also, following Etta Whyte's retirement. Etta had been connected with the shop for 25 years. And that summer, just one day before her 80th birthday, Miss Ingham died.

Miss Ingham had been 'a woman who sallies forth'. She had become a large woman who blamed her sturdy physique on the cakes offered to her by residents. 'I'm the size I am because I can't say "no"', she once said. It was a comment wholly at one with her overall approach to life and work. For Miss Ingham, observes Henry McIntosh, 'there was no such word as "no" or "can't". She would find a way to do anything'. It was an attitude that rubbed off on everyone who worked alongside her. She, as much as anyone, had defined the character of Viewpoint. On occasions, she had frustrated Norman and Board members alike. But the testimony of her assistant, Joan Marshall, shines through: 'I was richer for knowing her'. At the same time, Joan asks, did Viewpoint now need to be more organised? Were the days of 'being a family' numbered? Government policy of this period, and increasing scrutiny by public bodies, would suggest so, and Bob Duff, arriving in 1992 to take over where Norman Dunhill had left off, agreed.

Chapter 12

The importance
of partnerships

With the arrival of Bob Duff, and with Ian Penman now
at the helm of its Executive Committee, Viewpoint
moved rapidly to reposition itself within the social
housing sector, and to restore a good working
relationship with those public bodies (Scottish Homes in
particular) now responsible for funding social housing
and Homes.[171] The tone of the 1992–3 Annual Report is
determinedly cooperative, at times almost ingratiating,
reflecting the desire of the organisation to improve its
public standing.

> *We want to forge partnerships and co-operate with Local*
> *Authorities, social work departments, health boards and*
> *Scottish Homes in order that we can continue to provide a*
> *broad range of housing and care services for the elderly in*
> *need, particularly very Sheltered Housing. In that respect*
> *we welcome Scottish Homes' recent discussion paper,*
> *'Housing the Elderly in the 1990s', which places consid-*
> *erable emphasis on the need to make adequate housing*
> *and care provision for the rapidly expanding number of*
> *elderly people, particularly those over 85.[172]*

In the same report, Viewpoint's organisational structure
is clearly laid out, and placed with unequivocal clarity
below a list of statutory organisations with whom

Viewpoint intends to 'communicate effectively ... on a regular basis.' Again, Scottish Homes is listed alongside Local Authorities, health boards and social work departments.[173] 'Of great importance is the need for us to ensure that we complement their work and that our development strategies meet the needs they have identified.'[174]

The mood of necessary efficiency, and the explicit goal of a broad range of partnerships, has been quickly established, along with a style of management wholly new in Viewpoint's experience. Bob had come from the Anchor Housing Association (an off-shoot of Help the Aged), where he had been working as a regional director in the north east of England. He brought, in particular, experience of providing Extra Care housing for the frail elderly – which fed into Viewpoint's goal of continuous care provision. He also brought, arguably for the first time in Viewpoint's history, not only significant experience of another (and much larger) Housing Association's methods but also an outsider's clear-eyed perspective on the organisation – a quality that Ian Penman says the Committee was looking for at this time. Joan Stephenson, who would find the Association's new ways radically different from the approach of Norman Dunhill and Miss Ingham, nevertheless acknowledges that the 'sense of family' that had been one of Viewpoint's strengths might also have held it back from 'moving with the times.' Perhaps it needed an outsider like Bob to come in, she observes, in order to progress and survive.

In certain respects, Bob was a private man. He was an Ulsterman with personal experience of sectarian attitudes that may have helped shape a more reserved style than Viewpoint had thus far experienced in its chief executives. In Viewpoint, he also came up against a strong, and in its way feminist, tradition nurtured over many years by passionately committed, respectable Edinburgh ladies. Like Jack Fleming and others, Bob had to walk the unenviable tightrope of attempting to institute a modernising strategy without drawing down on his head the full wrath of the keepers of tradition. As Sandra Brydon observed, after being appointed Housing Manager four years later, Viewpoint was an organisation that 'struggled to move from a volunteer-based, benevolent style towards managing itself as a business.' How could it take on a business perspective without losing touch with its long-held values? There was, Bob believed, significant work to be done in order to review Viewpoint's structures and relationships. He would have known that any resulting changes could not be effected without churning up a degree of pain and anger.

Bob Duff's task was not made easier, however, by his decision not to live in Edinburgh but, rather, to commute on a weekly basis from his home near Newcastle. Many of the existing stalwarts of Viewpoint cared deeply not only about the Association but also about the city that it served. For some, Bob's decision seemed to symbolise a failure to love the organisation in the way they did. The decision masked his well-attested commitment to the new job. It perhaps reflected, also, an overall style that some experienced as less collaborative than they would have liked. The fact was, Bob Duff embodied necessarily new times and new priorities. His remit, recalls George Home – who would become Bob's Chairman – was quite clear: 'Rejuvenate Viewpoint or it will die.' Without the focussed determination he brought to the task of reviving funding sources, it is certain that Viewpoint's future would have been very different from the one it has now grown into.

Already in that 1993 Annual Report there are clear signs that Viewpoint was turning a corner in its relations with public funding bodies, and Ian Penman is clear that this was in no small measure due to Bob's ability to understand what it was they wanted from Viewpoint and to 'get close' to players of influence. The Committee was able to report that, following an absence of development funding from Scottish Homes, this year 'funds are on offer which should support us if we can make early progress with our site at St Stephen Place.' In fact, progress at that site would continue to be slowed down because of difficulties in purchasing the adjacent land. Nevertheless, at least Scottish Homes is now getting behind the plan, and three years on, Scottish Homes funding is expected not only for St Stephen Place but also for a long-standing Viewpoint project, Glenesk in Dalkeith.

Glenesk had been the family home of a local couple, Mr and Mrs Nimmo, They bequeathed it to Viewpoint Benevolent for the provision of housing in the Dalkeith area. Initially, Miss Ingham opened a small Residential Club, which ran for a number of years in the 1980s. However, the cost and upkeep of the house became unmanageable and it was decided to close the Club and lease the home to a family until such time that funds were in place to develop the site. This took time, and funding became available only after Viewpoint, under Bob Duff's guidance, forged local connections and obtained the Local Authority's support. In turn, the

Authority and Viewpoint made a joint case for funding to Scottish Homes. Because Glenesk was such a large and costly site to develop, Scottish Homes required that it be developed in three phases and provide a range of Extra-Sheltered and supported accommodation – an ambitious and complex arrangement that would take some fourteen years to complete. As ever, Viewpoint Trust was also signalling its support, having promised a further £100,000 of funding for the project.

What, other than the will to alter public perceptions of Viewpoint, was bringing about this apparent change of heart by Scottish Homes and others? A clue is in the language that we find being used by Viewpoint in the early 1990s. Again, the 1992–3 Annual Report is instructive. It speaks of the Government's Care in the Community policies and of the need for wardens and care staff to be trained in order to understand their roles, especially in relation to this new legislation. The Sub-Committee responsible for Viewpoint Homes notes with approval that training of nursing staff had been implemented prior to the most recent homes Inspections.[175] Training of wardens and other staff members is also highlighted in the 1995–6 report – sessions on Health and Safety for example. A 'thorough review' of financial procedures and systems has been undertaken. By means of training and review, there is a sense of standards being set across the organisation as a whole, demonstrating that Viewpoint is responding to legislative demands, and of a movement away from the culture of local autonomy that had given rise to difficulties in the past. Elisabeth Penman, an active member of Viewpoint committees during the 1990s, observes that the Housing Association movement in general was one that tended to attract employees at all levels, often of considerable character and imagination, who enjoyed the freedom of building their own small empires. It was a tendency that in Viewpoint, at least, was now being curtailed. The Association was shifting direction once again, and this time was ensuring that it did so in line with government policy and the expectations of its public paymasters.

The dominant approach to housing and care during the early 1990s was summed up in that phrase 'Care in the Community', the demands of which now began to influence strongly Viewpoint's move towards a longer term development strategy. Precisely what is meant by the phrase is not always entirely clear, it having been adopted by different groups and applied in different contexts. For example, the phrase reflects the fact that in the 1990s the proportion of adults heavily involved in providing care for close relatives increased. At the same time, it also conjures up headlines about the closure of old-style psychiatric hospitals and even high-profile incidents involving individuals who had been 'released' into the community. Broadly speaking, however, Care in the Community was an over-arching approach that was encapsulated in the NHS and Community Care Act 1990. It had to do with a move away from care within institutions to the provision of care and support services in the community. The ethos spawned new community services such as home treatment and outreach support teams, but it also drew on existing organisations, including Housing Associations, which were considered to be among those bodies that could help provide that support.

In response, said Riona Bell, Ian Penman's successor

as Chair of the Association, Viewpoint reviewed its Development Strategy and re-launched it in 1995 with an emphasis that reflects Government policy of the time:

> *It is clear that housing associations have a major role to play in providing accommodation for those returning to the community from long-stay hospital care and our Development Strategy now recognises that. Consequently, we now provide housing with care for a wider age range than previously ...*[176]

In the light of Care in the Community legislation, Viewpoint was now prepared to provide housing for those not of retirement age and, where appropriate, to adapt existing schemes to assist Care in the Community. Equally significant was that Viewpoint's response to the Care in the Community legislation provided the impetus and rationale for much of the new building and provision that the Association now undertook. The first such initiative was in an existing Viewpoint scheme, the notable 'Victorian industrial' building at Cameron Crescent. Here, a house was redeveloped, with part-funding from Scottish Homes, in order to accommodate five people returning to the community from Gogarburn Hospital (now closed but then offering a range of services in the area of mental health). To provide the kind of support required for the new tenants, Viewpoint worked in partnership with The Action Group. Likewise in Buckhaven, Fife, a detached family villa was converted at a cost of £237,000 to provide Care in the Community housing for five people from Lynebank Hospital in Dunfermline. Once again Scottish Homes part-funded the project and in this case, the relevant care would be provided by the Social Work Department and Fife Health Board.

These and other new projects were part of Viewpoint's determined efforts to put development back at the top of its agenda. In line with its revised strategy, the Association announced in 1997 that it had underway a £4.2 million development programme and had employed a former Scottish Homes employee, Susan Newman, to oversee it. 'The fact that this is happening', Sandra Brydon told residents, 'is a vote of confidence in us by Scottish Homes.'[77] The strategy also built upon Viewpoint's earlier decision to broaden its geographical range into Fife. This policy of expansion beyond Edinburgh had been taken with careful consideration, recalls Ian Penman (Chairman, 1991–2006).

There was by now an established aim within the Association of offering continuity of care for residents; a desire that no person should have to move from Viewpoint's care, or any great distance from their current residence, should their physical needs increase. But the Committee was anxious to avoid what he describes as a 'pepper pot approach'. Ian believed that by scattering residences throughout Scotland, as other Housing Associations had done, Viewpoint would make that eventuality more, not less, likely. He was concerned that building even on Viewpoint's interest in East Lothian (Prestonpans) and a developing interest out at Balerno (Lennox Tower) could produce precisely the 'pepper pot' approach he wished to avoid. The focus of Viewpoint's development, therefore, became concentrated north of the Forth bridges. By increasing its ability to offer various degrees of support within close proximity, Viewpoint could begin to guarantee the 'hierarchy' of care, of which Sheltered and Extra-Sheltered Housing were just two examples.

In 1997, work commenced on another project designed partly to offer Care in the Community provision in conjunction with Lynebank Hospital, this time 'The Vennel' in Dysart. This larger £2 million mixed scheme would comprise 31 units, the majority of which would be designed for older people (including a number with wheelchair access) but also including two shared housing units to accommodate eight individuals with learning needs, formerly resident at Lynebank. With their requirements in mind, a day centre was also included in the project design. Such facilities were intended to help the residents achieve greater independence than previously, allowing them to go out and to meet new people. The scheme, reported the project manager of Community Living Concepts, improved their quality of life 'with the wider range of opportunities on offer to them now.'[178] 'Dysart is just one of the specialist projects that we have provided in the past few years,' added Bob Duff. 'Our latest being two developments in Edinburgh, one [Drummond Place] for residents of Lynebank and the Royal Scottish National Hospital, Falkirk, who have family connections in Edinburgh. Living in the community has been welcomed by patients and their families and we hope to continue to provide housing for this vulnerable and needy group.'

Also in Dysart, Viewpoint continued what might be regarded as its more traditional work of managing Sheltered Housing, in this case a scheme of 31 units that had previously belonged to Scottish Homes. Scottish Homes had embarked on a 'stock transfer' initiative and Viewpoint was one of a number of Housing Associations that were bidding to take over the Dysart scheme during 1996. In the end, the decision would be made by the tenants themselves. They and the members of staff at Buchan Gardens were concerned about their future and the process of negotiation extended over several months. But it was in situations like this that Bob Duff came into his own. It brought out the salesman in him, recalls Ian Penman. Because of Viewpoint's ability to deploy private and charitable funds, Bob was able to lay considerable emphasis on the ability of Viewpoint Trust to pay for extras. What if the communal washing machine breaks down, asked the tenants. Viewpoint had the ability to respond, was the reply. We're in the business of raising standards, Bob told the residents, 'and we've got the Trust behind us'. It was, in many respects, the well-worn Viewpoint message and it was being preached once more to the traditional Viewpoint constituency. It worked. When it came to the final vote, 30 out of the eligible 31 residents voted and every one voted in favour of Viewpoint as their new landlord.

Not just in a 'selling' situation but also across the Association as a whole, attempts were being made to be more open with tenants and to build up a flow of information and feedback in both directions. The 1995-96 Annual Report contains a slightly awkward-sounding attempt by Bob to 'chat' to residents about a range of issues directly concerning them. He explains the difficulties faced by the Gardening Team and he invites tenants to become shareholders in Viewpoint at a cost of just £1.[79] This display of informality wasn't repeated in future Annual Reports, though communication through regular newsletters and the commissioning of tenant surveys was becoming an accepted part of Viewpoint life. The attempt to increase the number of tenant shareholders (again in line with the preferences of public bodies) did, however, yield fruit. The following year, Riona Bell reported that 143 tenants were now shareholders, making up 53 per cent of the total – a figure that steadily increased in succeeding years.

Within in the Residential Homes, also, there were renewed efforts to build a sense of community. Miss Elspeth Buchanan moved into St Raphael's when her mother died. Elspeth had worked as an artist and teacher all her life (latterly at Edinburgh's Cranley School for girls). In her room she points to the paintings on her walls. Two are striking portraits of her as a young woman, one by her mother and the other by her friend, the late Sir Norman Reid (Director of the Tate Gallery, 1964 – 1979) with whom she trained at the Edinburgh College of Art. Another student she met at the college was Miss Ingham.

Miss Buchanan came to St Raphael's thinking that she would work away quietly in her room. 'I thought I'd have every afternoon free. But after a while I had more of the philosophy of joining in with the staff's ideas'. She was delighted by the events organised by the Activities Organiser, appointed in 1997, at the encouragement of Lothian Social Work Registration, to work in the Residential and Nursing Homes. Annabelle Meredith (daughter of Scottish comic Chic Murray) developed a programme of tea dances, aromatherapy, outings and gentle exercises to music. 'Yoga – really PT.' says Elspeth. 'I remember her first talk. It was all about the disaster of the *Titanic!'*

In 1997, specialised care of another sort was also being acknowledged and rewarded. In that year Viewpoint received a Dementia Training Award, jointly sponsored by The Alzheimer's Disease Society and RSAS Age Care, and presented to staff at the Lennox House Nursing Home by the Duchess of Gloucester. Viewpoint was the only Housing Association in the UK to be recognised in this way that year. Because the award identified training undertaken by members of staff it acknowledged Viewpoint's commitment to staff training. But it also reflected the Association's long-standing awareness of the care required by those living with dementia. During her period as warden at Gillespie Crescent (1974–85), Marjorie Sinclair facilitated meetings designed to raise awareness of elderly needs. The increasing incidence of dementia was under discussion at that time, she recalls, and meetings attracted medical experts who would later specialise in this area. In England during the same period, Professor Tom Kitwood of the Bradford Dementia Group was another respected researcher pioneering appropriate care for what was a growing sector or the population. Indeed, research from the 1960s onwards was indicating, with significant consistency, that for those aged 65 and over 'the prevalence of dementia almost doubles in each five-year interval.'[180] In 1991, when Viewpoint was still looking to develop accommodation at Glenesk in Dalkeith, it was planned that the design would take into account the care and security of those living with dementia and Alzheimer's disease.

Similar attention to those with the greatest need

informed the work undertaken in the mid-1990s to revise the admissions policy (or 'Tenant Selection Policy'). There were those in the organisation who found the change of approach inherent in this work difficult to reconcile with what they considered to be the personal touch that Viewpoint had espoused. However, Viewpoint's traditional emphasis on building harmonious community had to be adapted to an environment in which government funding and monitoring was increasingly influential. Margaret Henderson remembers 'having to take more people on benefits', as opposed to 'retired gentlefolk' who could pay their own way. The formalisation of rules placed a far greater emphasis than before on the housing need of applicants and the priorities set by Local Authorities. The trick, as ever, was to maintain the Viewpoint ethos while satisfying legislative demands for clear and open procedures. That this careful balance was achieved is suggested by the way in which Viewpoint not only defined factors it would take into account when admitting a new tenant to its housing, but demonstrated its determination to go the extra mile, refusing to close waiting lists periodically as had been a regular occurrence in its own early days:

> *A current view held by some within the housing association movement is that visiting applicants is expensive and, because of insufficient vacancies, housing lists should be closed from time to time. However, Viewpoint believes housing associations have a duty to seek out and house those in most need and [that] to close housing lists (Registers of Applicants) discriminates against those who have not yet applied for housing. The closure of lists*

assumes that those already on the housing list are those in most need. Admittedly it is expensive to continue to visit new applicants but we believe that [this] is a cost that housing associations must bear if they are to identify those in most need.[181]

During the same year that the tenants of Buchan Gardens voted to be managed by Viewpoint, the Association also drew into the fold another Association that it had been instrumental in establishing – Croft-an-Righ. As a result, Croft-an-Righ underwent a major refurbishment, which transformed some of the accommodation into Extra-Sheltered units and added, among other facilities, the provision of a full meals service. Likewise, in May 1997 Kilravock also decided to 'transfer engagements' to Viewpoint, followed at the beginning of April 1998 by the Lennox Tower Housing Association based in Balerno. Each of these transfers brought not only new tenants under Viewpoint's care but also fresh faces to the committees. These included tenant representatives as well as those appointed for their experience and expertise. Just as Professor George Home moved over to Viewpoint when it merged with St Raphael's, so George Crainer joined Viewpoint courtesy of the amalgamation with Lennox Tower. Both Georges would eventually chair Viewpoint's Executive Committee.

In 1997, Viewpoint celebrated its 50th anniversary. Party buffets and birthday cakes were in constant supply that year, and residents took part in everything from traditional Scottish dancing to less traditional line-dancing. Celebrities were brought in to add sparkle to parties but at one celebration the guest of honour was a resident who had been a Viewpoint tenant for 49 years, almost from its inception.[182] At the same time, however, records begin to suggest another period of slowing down, a certain diminishment of the exuberance that had characterised the previous five years. News of building developments begins to be repeated rather than added to and a note of frustration creeps into even Bob Duff's public comments. In the Residents' Newsletter that reports the 50th anniversary celebrations, Bob expresses his disappointment with the discussions at Tenants' Forums. They are, he says, too much dominated with complaints about the gardens and not enough attention is paid to policy. Arguably, Bob's experience at these meetings was reflecting a growing disengagement with the Association as a whole by its tenants and residents. It was increasingly seen as a business by tenants, which made them disinclined to lend their support on a regular basis. The regularisation of fund raising through the more formal avenue of the Trust meant that the once fundamental marriage of fund raising and socialising was a thing of the past. Tenants were more independent and communal activity was in decline. Even trying to sell the annual Viewpoint Christmas cards around the projects was increasingly an uphill struggle, noted Joan Marshall.

Public funding, too, was creating headaches once more, this time because of the under-funding by government of the very policy to which Viewpoint had nailed its colours, Care in the Community. In his first year as Chairman, George Home writes:

The standards required by registration authorities are constantly increasing in terms of both personal and nursing care, and in terms of the physical standards of buildings. These result in increased costs but, regrettably, funding levels have not kept pace ... Funding levels have been frozen for the past two years, and in real terms this represents a funding reduction.[183]

The gap between the money made available for Care in the Community and Viewpoint's own costs was sufficiently wide to force Viewpoint (in contradiction to the principle it had laid out in its Admissions Policy) to limit its intake of residents who received state support. Professor Home indicated that the Association would emphasise the extent of its dilemma in its submission to the Royal Commission on Long Term Care of the Elderly. However, the Commission's Report did not, in Viewpoint's opinion, address this issue and, seven years later, George Crainer states in his final Annual Report that nothing has changed:

Each year I bemoan the fact that Care in the Community funding for certain of our care home residents is totally inadequate, which, in addition to having adverse financial consequences for Viewpoint, also restricts our ability to accommodate more Care in the Community funded residents than we do. It seems that the Scottish Executive does not listen to our pleas, and thereby makes life more difficult for those who must rely on Care in the Community funding.[184]

Now operating in this tightening financial environment, Viewpoint's decision to close the Ettrick Road Home the year following the 50th anniversary celebrations must have seemed to some like a shutting of the door on 'the old days'. Forever associated with Miss Ingham, the Pleiades and some of Viewpoint's most ambitious fund raising efforts, Ettrick Road was in some respects a symbol of what Viewpoint had stood for. But now the building didn't meet modern requirements and Viewpoint had to re-settle its residents elsewhere.

With hindsight, however, the transformation that the Ettrick Road Home underwent made it a new kind of symbol, this time of determination to meet changing, modern needs. Though initially unable to offer any guarantee that the building could be converted for other uses, Viewpoint proceeded in hope and developed proposals for numbers 12 and 14 Ettrick Road that would see them turned into a 'Vennel'-style mix of accommodation for older people and individuals returning to live in the community. It was a plan that would begin to come to fruition in 1999, with the support of Scottish Homes, together with the conversion on similar lines of another existing property, in Drummond Place. These conversions came at a time when once more Viewpoint was turning a corner, seeing a range of new projects underway or coming to a conclusion. Lade Court in Edinburgh's Stockbridge area offered a combination of sheltered and Extra-Sheltered Housing for frail older people, and Marian House in Oswald Road (adjacent to St Raphael's) was converted from an Extra-Sheltered scheme into an additional Residential Care Home.

In Fife, Viewpoint took over the old Hunter Hospital in Kirkcaldy, where it now operates supported housing as part of the Hunter House complex. In a scenario that echoes the story of City Park in St Andrews, the original home at the heart of the complex was built in 1786 as St Brycedale House for one, George Heggie. From 1896 to 1916 it was the home of Sir John Hunter who then bequeathed the house to Kirkcaldy as a hospital for the poor and incurably sick. In fulfilment of this bequest it served as the Hunter Hospital from 1936 to 1991. After the hospital's closure, the site lay empty for nearly a decade, any prospective buyer having to meet the terms of Sir John's original bequest, which was broadly interpreted as being for the health benefits of the people of Kirkcaldy. With the support of The Friends of Hunter Hospital, Viewpoint bought the site in partnership with Fife Special Housing Association. Under their plans, the 1950s additions to the original House were demolished and the main building converted in order to provide low-cost office space for not-for-profit organisations such as the WRVS. In the grounds, Viewpoint then built housing for older people and an additional eight-person unit for people living with dementia. Further complementary accommodation and facilities were built by Fife Special Housing Association. The nature of Viewpoint's contributions to the project meant that suitable government funds available for such a project could only be allocated to a private company. For that reason, and uniquely for the organisation, Hunter House was funded by Benview Trading Company, the company set up originally to operate Viewpoint's shops and now a wholly owned subsidiary of the Housing Association.

Finally, also, after years of waiting and negotiation, Viewpoint saw the completion of its large development at the 'Glenesk' site it held in Eskbank near Dalkeith. This was, Bob Duff would say, one of the achievements that he was most pleased about. The work had been developed over three phases, the last two beginning in 2001 and coming to fruition by the end of 2003. Three types of accommodation have been created: Extra-Sheltered accommodation within the old house itself, together with independent housing (the 'Railway Cottages') and, once more, Care in the Community Housing for people previously accommodated at Gogarburn Hospital.

On his appointment, Bob Duff had entered an organisation that was co-existing uneasily with the new demands being made by government and public funding bodies. He had been quite clear that his priority task was to rectify a situation which, if not addressed, might eventually leave the Association languishing in an untenable position. Development, he believed, was the key. Shortly before he left Viewpoint, he wrote in the tenants' magazine, *Newspoint*:

> *Housing associations are meant to offer an alternative to the private rented and Local Authority sectors, which of course necessitates developing new housing. Consequently, development is a core activity and an association without a development programme runs the risk of losing its impetus, and possibly its sense of direction also. A thriving or growing association attracts high calibre staff and committee members, so, in simple terms, one could say that growth equals success, and success attracts those staff and committee members who are most capable of delivering high quality services to you, the tenant.*[185]

The string of projects initiated during the years around the turn of the Millennium would argue that, notwithstanding the hiatus shortly after Viewpoint's 50th anniversary and despite the Care in the Community funding shortfalls reported by successive Chairmen, Viewpoint was indeed holding to Bob Duff's vision. Good quality housing was being developed for a wider range of clients than previously and by means of a widening range of effective partnerships; the Association's financial base was strengthening; and the organisation was growing rather than languishing. But there was a downside, too. In his farewell comments, Bob said that he would miss the staff and tenants of Viewpoint but that 'unfortunately I cannot say the same about the bureaucracy that the voluntary housing movement as a whole has had to cope with in recent years and which shows little sign of abating'.[186] It was a sad and barely oblique reference to the event that overshadowed the final months of Bob Duff's tenure as Director, the Pathfinder Inspection Report on Viewpoint carried out by Scotland's newest regulator of social housing, Communities Scotland.

The formation of Communities Scotland to take over responsibility from Scottish Homes was one aspect of the Housing (Scotland) Act 2001. The Act made a significant impact on the life of Housing Associations. It strove for consistency in tenants' rights and led to Viewpoint's own new tenancy agreement. It located funding for Associations within Local Authorities and at the same time imposed new responsibilities on them for preventing homelessness. This, noted Bob Duff, would probably mean that nominations and referrals would be made to housing providers such as Viewpoint, placing an additional pressure on its newly revised Allocations

Policy. More immediately, Viewpoint became one of the first Associations to come under the scrutiny of the Communities Scotland inspectors.

The inspection process overlapped coincidentally with an external Tenant Satisfaction Survey commissioned by Viewpoint. The Survey was overwhelmingly positive in its findings. Satisfaction with services, communication, repairs, local neighbourhoods, and with Viewpoint as a landlord, all registered in the high 90 per cent bracket. As an endorsement by the people it was serving, Viewpoint could hardly have hoped for better. The Communities Scotland Report, however, was another matter. Bob had been concerned that, this early in the life of its inspection process, Communities Scotland might have unrealistically high expectations of what were now termed Registered Social Landlords. He was worried that Viewpoint might suffer from the high ideals of inspectors not yet familiar with realities on the ground. Certainly, the sense of achievement that Viewpoint must have felt as a result of its recent growth is hardly evident in the final document. Viewpoint's confidence in its financial strength and the support of the Viewpoint Trust, and the evident expansion of its scope of activities, is largely ignored by the inspectors who speak instead of a lack of information that can be used to monitor and manage change. It concentrates on internal structures and systems, and the need to provide evidence for decisions at every level of the organisation. The Report argued that, while good work was being done, the Association was not in a position to demonstrate consistency and detailed evidence.

The Inspection Report made for a frustrating and

disheartening read. Many within the Association argued against the accuracy of some of its findings, but it was decided not to appeal. For Bob Duff, however, the Report was more than simply disheartening. It was a bruising response that set what he regarded as overly-bureaucratic structures against a decade of endeavouring to place Viewpoint on a secure footing. In the discussions that took place at committee level in response to the findings, Bob's voice slowly becomes silent. Photos of him over the years, especially when meeting residents – mingling with groups or presenting a trophy perhaps – convey the sense of a man with cheery confidence; the small photo used to illustrate his final letter to residents suggests instead a man who has been through several rounds in the boxing ring. Bob had had enough and he took the decision to retire.

Bob Duff's resignation coincided with the final report of George Crainer as Chairman of Viewpoint. He reflects on the preceding five years – on substantial growth in the Association's net assets, and on the government funding that has enabled Viewpoint to develop new schemes in Edinburgh, Fife and Midlothian. He doesn't mention the Inspection Report but notes that Viewpoint has introduced the extensive requirements of the Housing (Scotland) Act 2001 and points to the recent Tenants Satisfaction Survey as evidence of Viewpoint's high quality service to tenants and residents. He also poses a question, borrowed from a recent Scottish Federation of Housing Associations paper titled 'Sheltered Housing's Future'. Should Sheltered Housing move towards being 'retirement housing' with a property-based caretaking service or should it move towards a more highly supported type of provision, which can be a housing-based alternative to residential care? Viewpoint, we have seen, had developed experience over the years of both types of housing and care – with various options in between. But how would it move forward? It was a question to be answered by a new committee, a new Director and (for the first time since Miss Ingham stepped aside for Norman Dunhill) by *her* team.

Chapter 13

The changing shape of care

By the end of March, 2007, sixty years after its formation, Viewpoint was operating 29 housing and care complexes across the City of Edinburgh and in East Lothian, Midlothian and Fife. Altogether, 1,378 'units' of housing were registered with Communities Scotland. Of these, the largest number of units were categorised as Sheltered (549 in all) or Very Sheltered, also known as 'ExtraCare' (485). The remaining units were categorised as General (217), Medium Dependency (99) and units that facilitated wheelchair use (17). The greatest numbers of the Association's housing facilities were, as has always been the case, in Edinburgh,[187] making Viewpoint the largest provider of Sheltered Housing in the city. As it celebrates its Diamond Anniversary, therefore, Viewpoint is an Association of significant size, but one that remains relatively small compared with many of Scotland's other mainstream Registered Social Landlords, both in geographical reach as well as its tenancy numbers. Dunedin Canmore, for example, operates projects across a similar geographical area to Viewpoint but with well over double the number of units. Cairn Housing Association Ltd operates across Scotland as whole, and Port of Leith Housing Association operates in a small, focussed urban environment: both Associations operate over 2,000 registered units.

Where Viewpoint is distinctive is in the *range* of the housing it offers. The largest proportion of units belonging to Dunedin Canmore, Cairn, and Port of Leith (to take just those three examples) are all categorised as General Housing. Because of its longer history, as well as its roots in work with older, single women, Viewpoint has moved towards a wider range of Sheltered and Care Housing. Unusually, it also operates Care Homes, thus making it a broader-based, non-standard Registered Social Landlord. It has responded, and continues to do so, to social and legislative changes on two fronts: in the housing-for-rent market and in residential care. Changes in both areas arise, on the one hand, from evolving legislation and, on the other, the shifting expectations and demands of residents and their families. Informed by need and enforced by legislation, these drivers of change are undeniably interrelated and both equally important. In recent times, one of the demands that have made themselves heard most clearly is the desire for more spacious accommodation. The bed-sit arrangements that offered security and even a touch of luxury to the single women of Miss Cunningham's generation, and even Miss Ingham's, nowadays have little attraction. Potential residents have voted with their feet and bed-sit accommodation has been left lying empty. Viewpoint was in danger of falling behind the times – a fact also reflected in falling rental income. To address this situation, in 2006 Viewpoint embarked upon an ambitious £2.5 million programme of refurbishment – as explained through the tenants' magazine, *Newspoint*.[188]

The Viewpoint Management Committee had committed to converting the organisation's 170 'Studio

Flats' (or bed-sits) into individual, self-contained flats. One year later, in autumn 2006, *Newspoint* was able to report that a pilot phase of the conversion scheme had been completed at Ingham Court in Salisbury Road. As well as the residents themselves, it was not only Viewpoint that would benefit from these conversions, argued Housing Manager Sandra Brydon. In a letter to St Andrews Community Council, she explained that Viewpoint's City Park complex had been operating for some time with housing vacancies due to the low uptake in bed-sit accommodation. The conversions, together with additional flats, were intended to reduce the vacancies and aid the Local Authority to meet its housing needs by reducing its waiting lists.[189]

For the residents involved, some upheaval was inevitable. To facilitate the conversion work, they would have to move either temporarily, with a planned return to their original, refurbished flat, or – in some cases – permanently. 'I was happy with my studio', responded Mrs Janet Anderson from Inverard in Inverleith Gardens, 'and the prospect of moving home worried me at first and it was a great upheaval. However, when the move came around, I had to do very little as everything was taken care of. I am now very happy in my new home'.[190]

An event that caused a good deal more disquiet among residents, as well as catching the attention of the media, was the decision to review the delivery of dining room catering within Viewpoint's Extra-Sheltered accommodation. 'It was a shock to all of us', declares one resident, describing the loss of the service at Inverard House. '[The meals are] why a lot of people came here in the first place'. She speaks of fish suppers on a Sunday night, of being able to invite friends for meals – and of fighting hard to keep the service. But the fact was that the numbers using the catering service on a regular basis in Inverard had reduced to single figures, making the service uneconomical. 'If you don't use it, you lose it,' comments one resident. Sandra Brydon makes a similar point in her letter to St Andrews Community Council. At City Park, she writes:

> ... historically, there has been a very low take-up of this service. When we reviewed it as a part of a major review of Sheltered Housing services, we discovered that only six tenants were using it on a regular basis, that is other than casual users.[191]

Tenants had alternatives, she continues. The majority were cooking their own meals or receiving other kinds of assistance – meals on wheels or the delivery of frozen meals. Microwave ovens have played their part in changing what is possible and Local Authorities have developed their services for older residents. And there is a correlation, too, between the replacement of bed-sits with self-contained flats and the decline in communal dining. Older people are valuing their independence longer and, says Sandra Brydon, having worked all their lives, they want the kind of space and self-sufficiency that a thirty-year old can expect to achieve.

Nevertheless, this was an uncomfortable time. When one national newspaper got hold of the catering story, Sandra Brydon wrote in detail to residents, insisting that no tenant was being left to make alternative provision and that staff had worked closely with alternative catering providers and Local Authorities, the body finally responsible for ensuring provision of meals.[192] 'We do face many challenges and changes', she added, 'and that will bring about some anxieties for all of us.' Viewpoint's senior members of staff, charged with the delicate task of taking residents forward with the new living arrangements, remained acutely aware that they were dealing with emotive subjects, and that with older age and vulnerability can come growing fears and frustrations. 'Tenants have lost things that they had for years and valued', admits Chief Executive Margaret Wilkinson. 'It's hard for them to see the gains.'

Margaret Wilkinson succeeded Bob Duff in 2005. She was appointed with the task of helping Viewpoint address changing needs, government policies, Local Authority strategy, increased regulation and financial pressure – while at the same time remaining personally committed to 'keeping the past with us.' A qualified nurse and former ward sister, Margaret had spent 19 years working with the Church of Scotland's Board of Social Responsibility, now *CrossReach*. For the last two years of her time there, she was Head of Services to Older People, allowing her to come back, as she says, 'to one of my favourite client groups.'[193] The move to Viewpoint felt like a natural transition, but she and the new Chairman, Colin Sharp, were faced immediately not only with an unsettled climate for tenants but also unrest among members of staff. A tribunal process initiated by a group of Viewpoint wardens (echoing similar cases brought within the Local Authority sector at this time) asked whether women were receiving equal pay to men in the organisation – though not necessarily with men doing comparable jobs. As a result of the case, every job description within the organisation had to be rewritten and every salary reassessed – a lengthy one-and-a-half year process that Margaret describes as 'no less than traumatic. Morale dropped like a stone'. She describes a time in Viewpoint's history when, in common with other charitable organisations, much was agreed informally, on trust, or because it 'felt right', and compares this with a present day culture of continuous evaluation. Neither approach is without its difficulties, she concludes.

Viewpoint has not been alone in struggling, on occasions, to adjust to this climate of change. In 2008, Scottish Government Social Research published a study of the supply and condition of Sheltered Housing. Most providers of Sheltered Housing, it indicated, were having to respond to recent changes 'driven by a number of compelling and inter-related factors.'[194] High on that list of factors were the regulations, including the European Working Time Directive, that have brought about a radical reorganisation in warden services – universally the most unpopular culture change for residents of Sheltered Housing.

Over the four decades since Viewpoint started hiring wardens to be 'on hand' in quite an informal way, the role had become increasingly complex. Marjory Sinclair recalls a time when she would do her last round of the evening wearing hard-soled shoes, the theory being that just the sound of her walking the corridors gave residents a sense of security at night time. Common sense and simple solutions remain part of a good warden's armoury:

No longer just a 'good neighbour', the warden's role today

*is complex, demanding and time consuming. It is an
amalgam of manager, administrator, care co-ordinator,
counsellor, social secretary, first-aider, and being handy
with a screwdriver helps too. Chiefly though, a warden
needs to be a good communicator as a major part of the
job is that of care co-ordinator. You need to be able to
organise all available help and support services for
tenants when they need them (available in theory
anyway), so you need to know about, and be able to find
your way through, the network of support services, both
statutory and voluntary.*[195]

Within Viewpoint there has been a concerted effort over
the past decade to give greater recognition to this
evolving role, as well as clarity to the expectations
surrounding it. On her arrival as Housing Manager in
1996, Sandra Brydon had a sense that Viewpoint's forty
wardens were feeling disconnected from the rest of the
organisation. Many didn't know each other despite long
years of service. To the pressures of the job and a shifting
culture was added a degree of isolation. Under Sandra's
guidance, a Wardens' Forum was established and
networking teams were created. These allowed wardens
from different developments to work together, sharing
experiences and initiatives. Additionally, and for the first
time, a comprehensive Wardens' Procedures Manual was
created. It was intended to guide staff members but also
to inform residents and their families whose expectations, at times, could be unrealistic. (Even in 1998,
Marjory Sinclair was noting that 'relatives often think of
the warden as a nurse, which of course is not the case.'[196])

It is unsurprising that expectations have had to be

reassessed during this period, given the changes to the context in which residents live and wardens work. People continue to live longer than before, but the accompanying tendency towards supporting people to live in their own homes for as long as possible has meant that when older people do move to Sheltered Housing, they are often more frail than was once the case. They often bring with them complex issues related to dependency and dementia. Inevitably, this has placed more demands on wardens and squeezed budgets yet more tightly.

One of the factors affecting budgets has been a rise in costs stemming from the European Working Time Directive, which came into effect in October 1998 and increased the amount of paid leave to which care staff members were entitled. The same Directive, together with other legislation, also brought a change to wardens' terms and conditions, moving them from a commitment of 21 hours 'on call', six days per week, to something approaching nine-to-five office hours. Relatives who visited one former Viewpoint resident in the 1980s recall their great appreciation of the diligent way in which wardens 'worked round the clock'. But they admit to 'the uneasy feeling' they had at the time that wardens were being exploited.

Now, wardens were no longer required to live on site and could operate their 'on call' shifts from home. Once again, for older residents, this change has been perceived as a reduction in service, an erosion of their feelings of security and yet one more scenario to which they have had to adjust. Viewpoint, like other organisations with wardened facilities, has had to reassure its residents and address that sense of loss.[197]

So what of the positive outcomes that these changes have brought? Over time, argues Susan Brydon, wardens have been positioned more securely within the established culture of community care, which has increasingly come to acknowledge wardens as the professionals they are alongside other members of the caring and social work professions. 'Previously, healthcare and social care workers made decisions about older residents without including wardens in the process of assessing need.'[98] Now the skills and knowledge described by Marjory Sinclair are adding in a more sustained and valued way to the task of community care.

Closely related to these developments in staffing hours and practices – and in some cases making them possible – have been improvements and innovations in support technology. 'Inactivity monitoring' is one example. Where once a mat concealed beneath an ordinary rug would transmit a signal to the warden's office indicating whether a tenant had been moving about the flat in the past few hours, now an infra-red detection system is linked to a call-centre, from which the appropriate people can be contacted if a tenant's flat seems unusually still. Similarly, alarm systems within Viewpoint properties are connected to a central call-centre. The Scottish Government Review noted that 'many [residents] were reluctant to use the community alarm systems.'[99] However, Isabella and James Glass, residents at Woodthorpe in Colinton, speak of being reassured about the system following an organised visit arranged by Viewpoint to the Hanover Telecare Centre in McDonald Road. Here, they discovered that all the relevant files required in an emergency could be called up on the Hanover computers without their situation having to be explained over the phone. Moreover, first-hand experience of the system came one night when James was taken ill unexpectedly. 'They knew who we were and had all our medical details,' says Isabella, 'and within half an hour of phoning we were in the Infirmary.'

The adjustments and new arrangements made in response to the wealth of changes instituted over recent years have varied across Scotland's Housing Associations. Viewpoint's approach has been to rethink completely what it provides and where. All of the factors described in this chapter – the demand for one-bedroom flats, the developing technology and change in the practice of wardens – have been brought to bear in a re-categorisation of all Viewpoint's properties. It reflects not only the new approaches to housing care but also the continuing range of what Viewpoint offers. Three categories have been established:

– *Alarmed serviced housing with remote monitoring*
– *More traditional Sheltered/Retirement Housing (with on-site staff support)*
– *Enhanced Supported Housing (with on-site staff and additional services)*

At the same time, the impact of demand and legislation that has so altered the outward appearance of Viewpoint's housing provision has had an equally dramatic effect in the field of Care Home provision. Here, says former Director of Community Services, Jane Douglas, Viewpoint has been leading the way. Prior to 2001, Nursing Homes had been registered with the Health

Board and Residential Homes with the Social Work Department. After 2001, both kinds of Home were brought together under the auspices of the Care Commission and designated 'Care Homes'. The property at Inverleith Terrace was sold off with great regret in 2005. It had proved too difficult to upgrade to the required modern standards and so the majority of residents were moved into two of Viewpoint's three remaining Care Homes: St Raphael's and Marian House. The third Care Home currently operated by Viewpoint is Lennox House, the 'Club' originally established though the endeavours of Miss Ingham and Viewpoint Benevolent. The delivery of care in all three Homes has been re-shaped in the light of this change but most especially as a result of the growing recognition that 'getting old is not an illness and most health care needs don't require a nurse.'[200] In terms of the atmosphere and staffing of a Care Home, this is a more radical statement than it may at first appear. It is no longer a requirement that a Home be staffed with a nurse at all time. As in hospitals, the roles formally attributed solely to nurses may be taken by others and what Viewpoint has championed is the desire to give residents of Care Homes the kind of support they need *all* the time, not just occasionally. In Marian House, for example, where 70 per cent of residents are living with dementia, it is specialised dementia care that is most needed.

Making the environment appropriate for residents has required getting the correct balance of staffing, which Jane insists was not reassessed as a cost-cutting exercise but in order to enhance the quality of care. She enthuses about the Government's 1994 White Paper entitled *Houses are for Living*: 'we all believe in that – in people-centred care. My ideal is for it to be a positive experience moving out of your home into a Viewpoint Care Home'. It's an ideal that spans the full range of Viewpoint's housing and care complexes. Typically, Jean Simpson, warden of Inverard Sheltered Housing, speaks of encouraging one woman who had not yet retired from her job to think not so much of moving into Sheltered Accommodation as into 'a new home that you like and which, when the time is right, will provide you with support and services that are helpful to you'.

Viewpoint's aim now, as in the days of Miss Cunningham, is to create a 'home from home'. Jane describes as an inspiration the goals of the Eden Alternative care organisation, which are 'based on the core belief that aging should be a continued stage of development and growth, rather than a period of decline'. It is:

> *committed to de-institutionalising the culture and environment of today's Nursing Homes and other long-term care facilities [and] dedicated to eliminating the plagues of loneliness, helplessness, and boredom that make life intolerable in most of today's nursing homes.*[201]

In 'de-institutionalising the institution', Viewpoint now talks about 'the House' and not 'the Home'; and not of 'domestics' but of 'house-keepers' (who, says Jane, often have special, caring relationships with residents). In meeting individual preferences, staff can also make a resident's experience more personal and satisfying. 'If a person wants to have a croissant for breakfast then that's what he should have. It's important that you get what you want. You would in your own home or in a hotel.'

Jane sees this focus on the individual as the approach that will continue to inform the re-shaping of Viewpoint's Care Home style. She envisages, for example, a time when a relative can make a cup of tea with a resident who is living with dementia rather than being served by a member of staff. In this way, both resident and visiting relative are doing something together that they have been used to doing previously. And if more facilities or equipment are required to enable this possibility, then so be it. 'It isn't expensive to do,' she says. 'We could fund raise for it.'

'We could fund raise for it ...' Suddenly, with those few words, Jane echoes and encapsulates all the commitment and determination that has characterised Viewpoint over the past sixty years. Though the outward shape of care for older people continues to change – and arguably faster even than in Norman Dunhill's day or Miss Ingham's – Viewpoint holds on to its belief not only that 'where there's a will there's a way' but also, crucially and fundamentally, in the importance of the individual.

Chapter 14
Viewpoint in the future

In its pursuit of dignity, privacy and personalised care for its tenants and residents, Viewpoint in the first decade of a new Millennium continues to uphold values that would have been recognised by Miss Cunningham and her committee of 'like-minded women'. In 1947, Viewpoint was offering a rare housing alternative to older, single women at a time when the only option for many old people was to live out the end of their lives in the workhouse. For all the early difficulties of communal living, the residents of Anne, Bridget and Charlotte Houses were given an opportunity to live independently and not simply to 'exist' institutionally. And there remains a direct connection between that pioneering, radical possibility and the present-day commitment within Viewpoint's Care Homes to 'de-institutionalise the institution'. The Care Homes themselves, and the Guest House Homes that preceded them, represent a widening of Viewpoint's goals and illustrate the organisation's continuing endeavours to raise its own standards of housing and care and demonstrate to others what can be done. As the previous chapter showed, this work is carried out in response to, and sometimes in the face of, a wide diversity of factors. Economic conditions, government policy and the aspirations of prospective residents all play their part. So, too, do developing technology and the need, by any service organisation, to offer value for money. But driving all these factors relentlessly is the changing demographic of the British population.

This is not only a question of age. The Tenants' Handbook produced in 2008 includes introductory paragraphs in Polish and Mandarin, reflecting just two of the distinctive communities that have become well established since the post-war years within Edinburgh's social mix. Nevertheless it is undoubtedly our ability to live longer that lies behind much of the social change to which Viewpoint must respond. The Wanless Social Care Review published in 2006 (*Securing Good Care for Older People: taking a long-term view*) reported that in the next twenty years, the number of people aged over 85 would increase by two-thirds compared with just a ten per cent growth in the overall population. At the same time, it was expected that the total number of people with disabilities in later life, and potentially in need of care, will be higher, thus increasing the demand for social care and putting further pressure on available resources and funding.[202]

To put some numbers on that statistic, between 1999 and 2056 the segment of the UK population aged 85 and over was projected to rise from 1.1 million to 3 million – though 'official population projections have frequently underestimated improvements in life expectancy'.[203] One predicted result of this rise is that 'the number of elderly and physically disabled people living in one sort of residential setting or another should peak at just under 1 million in the mid-2000s, compared with 480,000 in 1999.'[204]

The figures predicted vary from year to year but the

trend observed by Marjory Sinclair and feared by Norman Dunhill continues unabated. As a result, there is an imperative in general to build more housing and create more care spaces for older people. For Viewpoint, in particular, there is also a need to build 'merely to stand still'.[205] In part, as Bob Duff had observed, this is because an organisation that does not grow cannot change and without change it is more likely to wither and die. More immediately, one effect of upgrading Viewpoint's 'studios' to one-bedroom flats has been to reduce the income available from each property. Simply to counter that effect, Viewpoint needs to create more housing opportunities. However, Housing Associations caring for older people are not the only ones who want to build more properties and it is worth pausing to assess the environment within which Viewpoint now endeavours to look to the future.

In present-day Britain, it is not only the elderly who require more housing. There is a demand for more housing in general, a fact that the Labour Government set out to address when Gordon Brown became Prime Minister in 2007:

> *In two eras of the last century - the interwar years and the 1950s onwards – Britain made new housebuilding a national priority. Now through this decade and right up to 2020 I want us – in environmentally friendly ways, using principally brownfield land and building eco towns and villages – to meet housing need by building over a quarter of a million more homes than previously planned, a total by 2020 of 3 million new homes for families across the country.[206]*

While many welcomed Mr Brown's announcement, there were also those who felt that the Government's commitment to building more affordable housing for people to buy and rent was inadequate. They pointed to the 1.5 million people on waiting lists and the fact that in England only 300 new council houses had been built in the previous year. The housing charity Shelter argued that the new push for affordable housing was required largely to reverse the impact of the Conservative Government's 'right to buy' policy, which had resulted in one-third of the UK's six million council houses being sold off.[207]

An identical picture was painted in Scotland: promises of increased housing and demands for more affordable housing for rent. For the Scottish Government, the desire to build new homes was seen as a method of maintaining the nation's 'economic competitiveness.' Shelter Scotland and the Chartered Institute of Housing argued that building even substantial numbers of new houses would not have the effect of making them affordable for large numbers of Scottish families. 'One in three working families in Edinburgh is unable to buy the cheapest property available as the affordability gap has widened sharply since 2000', reported *The Scotsman*. 'It's clear', responded Shelter Scotland, 'that building more new houses for sale cannot be the only answer.'[208]

Across the UK, Housing Associations are seen by Government as having an important role in meeting this demand for more affordable housing. Associations already almost equal Local Authorities in the amount of housing that they own,[209] a very different picture from when Viewpoint embarked on its Sheltered Housing programme in the mid 1970s. Professor Kenneth Gibb summarises how, in Scotland, the situation has changed since then, comparing the work of Housing Associations with that of council housing:

> *In retrospect the 1970s was the high watermark of council housing before the tide of 2 million council house sales [under Mrs Thatcher's Conservative Government] and deep sustained spending cuts changed things forever. In 1971, housing associations, voluntary sector not for profit landlords, hardly registered. Enabling legislation in 1974 and 1988 along with policies to transfer public housing, plus the decision to channel social housing new build through the association sector – helped grow the successful Scottish housing association sector. Relative and absolute growth continued through the 1990s. Associations are now (end 2005) 40% plus of all social housing in Scotland. In 1993 they were less than 10%.* [210]

What some observers also perceive, however, is not only the continuing and inevitable pressure on Housing Associations to build more housing but the resulting difficulty that some Associations now find in maintaining their sense of identity and raison d'être. 'Housing Associations are still overwhelmingly registered as charities, but their links with the past can appear tenuous as they morph into full-blown development "companies" ... [helping] deliver perhaps a third of the 3 million new homes Gordon Brown targeted for completion by 2020', wrote Peter Hetherington in *The Guardian*.[211] He quotes the Director of Shelter's concern that the Housing Association movement is becoming fragmented and 'being pulled inexorably away from worrying how the poor and dispossessed get housed ... [At] the margins they are beginning to become less like charities and increasingly indistinguishable from private corporations.'[212]

To a certain extent, this is nothing new. The evolving relationship with government is an important theme running through any history of Housing Associations. Viewpoint's own Ian Penman notes that during his time as Chairman a good number of Committee members were former civil servants, 'and this was pretty much accepted. It reflected the fact that Housing Associations were an off-shoot of government and that government was backing them'. It was a situation that his successor, George Home, found frustrating. He was anxious for a more business-led approach and encouraged Bob Duff accordingly. James Tickell summarises the situation:

> On the one hand, there is the natural urge for govern-
> ments to regulate, control, direct and create obedient
> instruments for delivery of government policy. On the
> other, there is the independence of housing associations,
> their entrepreneurial qualities, their creativity and their
> own social purposes. Here ... there can never be a final
> resolution to the issue, rather an ever-evolving set of
> compromises.[213]

Within this broad environment of an aging population and the pressure, from a multiplicity of directions, for new housing, Viewpoint in 2008 sees itself determinedly holding to its core purpose of providing social housing and continuing care primarily (though not exclusively) to older people. 'We want to take away the worries of those growing old; pursue strategies of innovation, flexibility and adaptability; become the provider of choice; modernise our practices in housing and care; and meet the changing expectations of our customers.'[214]

In its plans for the future, Viewpoint is looking to undertake work that is sustainable and 'doable'. This includes developing the amount of property that it can make available for Sheltered and supported housing, but that task is not easy in the current climate. Land within Viewpoint's traditional geographical radius, especially within Edinburgh itself, is only available at a premium. Moreover, Housing Associations are often treated in exactly the same way as private for-profit developers, sometimes having to contribute from their own funds to non-housing facilities in return for being able to build on Local Authority land.[215] Nevertheless, Viewpoint continues to develop. In December 2006, it opened Harbour House in Kirkcaldy. This Victorian property, once the home of a tea and wine merchant, has been converted with the guidance of Historic Fife. It now consists of six general needs flats to add to Viewpoint's growing presence in the 'Kingdom of Fife'.

In order to grow further, Viewpoint is clear about the need to work in partnership with other appropriate organisations. Already it is a member of the Rowan Group, a partnership of seven Edinburgh-based Housing Associations that work together to apply for project funding from Edinburgh City Council. The all-important 'HAG money' (Housing Association Grant funding) available for the kind of work Viewpoint plans is distributed by the Scottish Housing Regulator (the successor body to Communities Scotland) through local councils. At the present time, Edinburgh Council's preferred policy is to work with a group of providers rather than with Associations on an individual basis. The Rowan Group has been successful in its bids, says Margaret Wilkinson, but she also knows that future success will depend in part on even closer ties and mergers with other housing and care providers. In today's shifting economy, a larger overall organisation is in a better position to make the savings that, in turn, place it in a better position to develop as it hopes to.

In particular, Viewpoint is keen to build upon its proven expertise in the field of dementia care. One option is to develop Sheltered Housing in such a way that it is designed to cope with the onset of dementia. At the moment, it is not always possible to provide the appropriate care, as Dan Orr explains. He and his wife moved into Inverard House in 2001 in part because his wife had developed Alzheimer's disease, and here was a place that offered them both support, including the provision of communal meals. It was a difficult move to make, one which Dan says dragged his own health down, but it worked for a number of years. As the condition of Dan's wife deteriorated, it was then decided that she should move to Viewpoint's Care Home at Lennox House and this, too, worked for a while. However, eventually, Dan's wife's condition meant that Dan had to make the decision for her to be moved to other purpose-built accommodation designed for those with memory loss. It's a difficult scenario that Margaret Wilkinson understands. Many members of Viewpoint's staff have relatives living with dementia, she says, and the question is simple: 'What would we want?' As result, Viewpoint is working closely with the Dementia Services Development Centre at Stirling University to remodel its approach to dementia care in the light of new possibilities. For example, Margaret envisages as one solution the development of 'Care Villages' – a concept already pioneered in England and one that echoes both the driving motivation behind Viewpoint's Target £1 Million Fund in the 1980s and also the St Raphael's-Kilravock development of the 1990s. The idea of placing a range of housing and care facilities side by side would ensure not only that Viewpoint tenants don't have to move outwith the organisation for the additional care that dementia demands; neither would they have to move from their immediate environment. Couples such as Dan and his wife should be cared for together despite their diverging needs.

This continuing desire to explore a diversity of housing and care options is one of Viewpoint's defining characteristics[216] and is – as it has always been – a pragmatic response to the rapidly changing world of social housing and care. Nowhere is that change more evident than in the idea embedded in government policy over the past decade, that older people should be cared for in their own homes for as long a possible:

> *Most older people prefer to receive care at or close to home, and there is evidence that greater emphasis on respite care, day care and social work would improve outcomes. For people with low levels of need, there is some evidence that social care, often provided in the community, can delay the use of more intensive services such as nursing home care.*[217]

This is yet another area to which Viewpoint is now turning its attention and, in doing so, re-thinking the best way to use its existing resources. Until recently, up to 90 per cent of Viewpoint's services have been offered on its own premises.[218] Although Miss Ingham would have argued vociferously that the organisation was not about 'bricks and mortar', nevertheless for the first sixty years of its existence, Viewpoint's work has been most clearly visible through what is offered within its buildings. Now, as Scotland's older people live longer, and with hopes for continuing independence, Viewpoint is addressing what are termed 'lifestyle services'. These are services that those living in their own homes require but find difficult to manage themselves, the kinds of day-to-day needs that can be met by gardeners, handymen and domestics.

In developing the provision of such services, there are potential benefits for Viewpoint itself, which currently employs large numbers of agency workers to fill a variety of roles. By building up its own 'labour agency', Viewpoint envisages creating a bank of part-time, flexible employees who can be assigned roles not only within its own properties when needed, but can also offer the services required by older people living in their own homes. As a result, Viewpoint would be bringing in-house part of the spending currently put out to other agencies, earn some income for its own charitable purposes and, at the same time, establish its own structures of quality control. The new project will be managed through Benview Trading Ltd, the company originally set up to manage income from Viewpoint's successful charity shops. In recent years, Benview has had little activity to oversee, except for the management of Hunter House in Kirkcaldy. This new proposal, therefore, sets out not only to meet a growing need but also to offer an innovative modern-day successor to Viewpoint's earlier fund raising activities – illustrating once again the organisation's ability to pursue necessary change while maintaining an important degree of continuity with the past.

Viewpoint's development of 'lifestyle' service for older people is just one more example of the organisation's 60-year-old ability to re-shape services according to changing needs. In doing so, it sees its own members of staff, whether permanent or contract, as the crucial means of delivering those services. Members of the Viewpoint Board, together with Margaret Wilkinson and her senior staff, are determined to nurture Viewpoint's staff through continuing learning and development and, in so doing, help them to stay within the organisation and advance its reputation for expertise. In securing and celebrating its position as Scotland's oldest Housing Association, Viewpoint aims only for the best; to be a model for excellence and a provider of excellence. Miss Cunningham could have asked for nothing more.

Appendix 1
Sources

SELECTED BIBLIOGRAPHY

Mary Campion *Place of Springs: the story of the first 100 years of the province of the Maternal Heart of the Little Company of Mary* (1977: The Way Publications)

Karen Croucher et al *Review of Sheltered Housing in Scotland* (2008: Scottish Government Social Research, www.scotland.gov.uk/socialresearch)

Richard J Finlay *Modern Scotland 1914–2000* (2004: Profile, London)

Charles McKean *Edinburgh: an illustrated architectural guide* (1982: Edinburgh, Royal Incorporation of Architects in Scotland, 3rd edition 1983)

Peter Malpass *Housing Associations and Housing Policy: a historical perspective* (2000: Palgrave Macmillan, London)

David Thomson *England in the Twentieth Century* (1965: Penguin, Harmondsworth)

James Tickell *Turning hopes into homes: a short history of affordable housing* (2005: National Housing Federation, London)

Derek Wanless et al *Securing Good Care for Older People: taking a long-term view* ('Wanless Social Care Review') (2006: King's Fund, London)

KEY DOCUMENTS FROM THE VIEWPOINT ARCHIVES

J M M Cunningham *Autobiography* (undated manuscript)

Susan Maclennan *Viewpoint Housing Association, 1947–97* (1997: Viewpoint, unpublished). Incorporates less complete account begun by Miss Ingham.

INTERVIEWS

Ms Sandra Brydon, Director Housing Services, 1996 ff.

Miss Elspeth Buchanan, Resident, St Raphael's

Ms Jane Douglas, Director of Community Services 2005–07

Mr Norman Dunhill, Director of Viewpoint 1975–92

Mr Jack Fleming, Chairman, 1985–91

Mr and Mrs J Glass, Tenants, Woodthorpe

Mrs Margaret Henderson, Resident, St Raphael's

Professor George Home, Chairman, 1997–2001

Mrs Muriel (Peggy) Home, Volunteer, Stockbridge Budget Shop

Mrs Joan Marshall, Member of staff, 1979–2007

Mrs Hilda McCoy, Tenant, Croft-an-Righ

Mr Henry McIntosh, Director, Central Services 1991–2007

Mrs Susan Maclennan, Housing Officer, 1985–92

Mrs Meg MacNeill, Resident, Inverard

Miss Moira Milne, Resident, Inverard

Mr Dan Orr, Resident, Inverard

Mr Ian Penman, Chairman, 1991– 2006

Mrs Elisabeth Penman, Former Volunteer and Committee member

Miss Jean Simpson, Warden, Inverard 2003 ff.

Mrs Marjorie Sinclair, Warden, 1975–2007

Mrs Joan Stephenson, Housing Manager, 1975–1996

Mrs Etta Whyte, Convenor, Tanfield Budget Shop 1967–92

Mrs Margaret Wilkinson, Director of Viewpoint, 2005 ff.

Appendix 2
Chairs and Senior Officers

Viewpoint Housing Society 1947–72

CHAIRS

1947–58 Miss Jane M M Cunningham
1958–63 Miss C M Rankine Brown
1963–72 Miss Elizabeth R Cockburn

OFFICERS

1947–52 Miss Muriel S Ellis (Secretary/Manager)
1952–72 Miss Ann Evelyn Ingham (Secretary/Manager)

Viewpoint Housing Association 1972–91

CHAIRS

1973–77 Miss Elizabeth R Cockburn
1977–78 Mr George D Cheyne
978–85 Lady Antonia Avonside
1981–85 Mr John (Jack) Fleming

Viewpoint Benevolent 1972–91

CHAIRS

1977–78 Mr George D Cheyne
1977–79 Miss Elizabeth R Cockburn
11985–91 Mr John (Jack) B Fleming
1985– *have asked Ross Oliver to help me out on this*

OFFICERS

1972–75 Miss Ann Evelyn Ingham (Secretary/Manager)

1975–91 Mr Norman Dunhill (Director)

1975– 87 Miss Ann Evelyn Ingham (Secretary/Manager)

1987–91 Mr Norman Dunhill (Secretary/Manager)

Viewpoint Housing Association 1991–

CHAIRS

1991–2006 Mr Ian D. Penman

1996–97 Ms Riona Bell

1997–2001 Professor George Home

2001–06 Mr George Crainer

2006– Mr Colin Sharp

OFFICERS

1991–92 Mr Norman Dunhill (Director)

1992–2005 Mr Robert (Bob) Duff (Director)

2005– Mrs Margaret Wilkinson (Chief Executive)

Appendix 3

Notes

Chapter 2 A very particular need

1 *Christian Science Monitor* August 9, 1946, p.10

2 Richard Finlay *Modern Scotland 1914–2000* (2004: Profile, London), p.201

3 Finlay p.47

4 David Thomson *England in the Twentieth Century* (1965: Penguin, Harmondsworth) p.69

5 Finlay p.83

6 Thomson p.218

7 Finlay p.197

8 Peter Malpass *Housing Associations and Housing Policy: a historical perspective* (2000: London, Macmillan) pp.20-1

9 *Christian Science Monitor* op.cit

10 WS: Writers to Her Majesty's Signet. The WS Society is Scotland's independent association for lawyers and one of the oldest professional bodies in the world.

11 ibid

12 Malpass p.49

13 Estimate by Henry McIntosh, interviewed June 7, 2007

14 James Tickell *Turning hopes into homes: a short history of affordable housing* (2005: London, National Housing Federation) p.2

15 Tickell p.3

16 ibid

Chapter 3 Miss Cunningham

17 Jenni Murray, '20th Century Britain: the Woman's Hour' (2001: www.bbc.co.uk/history/british/modern/jmurray_01.shtml)

18 William Ewing (ed.) *Annals of the Free Church of Scotland, 1843–1900, Volume 1(Ordained Ministers and Missionaries)* (1914: Edinburgh, T&T Clark) p.131

19 ibid, *Volume 2 (History of the Congregations)* p.8

20 J M M Cunningham. 'Autobiography' (undated: manuscript) p.1

21 'An Edinburgh citizen remembers', *The Christian Science Monitor*, August 11, 1952

22 *The Christian Science Monitor* Aug 9, 1946, p.10

23 In Viewpoint's first Register of Members, Miss Georgina Hamilton Paterson and Miss Mora Johnston Stewart both have their occupation recorded as 'Christian Science Practioner'.

24 J M M Cunningham, 'Autobiography' (undated: manuscript) p.9

25 J M M Cunningham, 'Where the heart's eye turns' (1966: manuscript)

26 J M M Cunningham, "Sheep and Shepherds' (1963: manuscript)

Chapter 4 The alphabet houses

27 *The Illustrated London News* at www.iln.org.uk

28 *The Guardian*, November 17, 2007

29 Val Horsler *Elizabeth and Philip: 20 November 1947* (2007: London, National Archives) pp.7&88

30 www.eif.co.uk/G11_History.php

31 Un-attributed newspaper article, Viewpoint archives (Autumn 1947)

32 'Eve's Circle', *Edinburgh Evening News*, January 15, 1948

33 *Edinburgh Evening News*, January 15, 1948

34 'Eve's Circle', *Edinburgh Evening News*, date?

35 Unidentified newspaper article, September 27, 1948

36 Unattributed news cutting, Viewpoint archives

Chapter 5 So much so cheaply

37 'Eve's Circle', *Edinburgh Evening News*, date?

38 *The Scotsman* August 20, 1951

39 ibid

40 *The Scotsman* September or November 28, 1949

41 Alison Settle, 'Woman's Viewpoint', *The Scotsman*(?), undated

42 Minutes, Seventh Annual General Meeting, March 9, 1954

43 Minutes, October 31, 1950

44 'Eve's Circle', *Evening News*, 1949, undated

45 Minutes, Fourth Annual General Meeting, February 20, 1951

46 Alison Settle, 'Woman's Viewpoint', op.cit

47 ibid

48 Minutes, Fourth Annual General Meeting,
    February 20, 1951

49 'Eve's Circle', *Evening News*, undated 1949

50 Miss Ingham's unpublished history of Viewpoint, p.2

51 Minutes, January 3, 1952

52 Minutes, November 28, 1950

53 Minutes, December 12, 1953

54 Minutes, November 28, 1950

Chapter 6 Four Freedoms

55 Minutes, February 4, 1952

56 Annual General Meeting, February 20, 1951

57 ibid

58 'Eve's Circle, May 29, 1951

59 Minutes, February 4, 1960

60 Miss Rankine Brown had been one of Scotland's first
    women graduates. Miss Inglis states that she studied at
    Edinburgh University, but had to go to England in order to
    get her degree. (Notes from interview with Miss Inglis by
    Susan Maclennan, c.1996)

61 Minutes, March 8, 1960

62 ibid

63 Minutes, April 2, 1960

Chapter 7 Miss Ingham

64 Minutes, January 14, 1952

65 Minutes, November 15, 1951: 'Miss Cunningham asked the
    Committee to consider affiliating to the National Council of

Women, but as no member of the Committee was in favour of doing so, the matter was dropped.'

66   Minutes, February 4, 1952

67   Minutes, Sixth Annual General Meeting, February 24, 1953

68   Minutes, Sixth Annual General Meeting, February 24, 1953

69   Minutes, October 25, 1951

70   'Eve's Circle', *Evening News* undated

71   Minutes, Eighth Annual General Meeting, March 8, 1955

72   'Early days to 1972', text of a talk by Miss Ingham, undated

73   Minutes, June 19, 1954

74   *Edinburgh Evening News*, April 20, 1956

75   *Edinburgh Evening Dispatch*, November 2, 1956

76   *Edinburgh Evening News* ibid

77   ibid

78   Malpass p.130

Chapter 8 Making a community

79   Minutes, Ninth Annual General Meeting, March 27, 1956

80   Minutes, September 18, 1956

81   Minutes, April 12, 1957

82   'Viewpoint Benevolent', publicity brochure, undated

83   Minutes, June 26, 1959

84   Minutes, Tenth Annual General Meeting, April 16, 1957

85   Minutes, January 28, 1958

86   Minutes, February 22, 1957

87   Minutes, October 31, 1950

88   Minutes, October 22, 1951

89   ibid

90   Minutes, October 31, 1950

91   Minutes, November 19, 1960

92   Minutes, December 8, 1953

93   Minutes, November 27, 1956

94   See Chapter 12

95   Interview, Ian and Elizabeth Penman, October 3, 2007

96   Notes from interview with Miss Inglis by Susan Maclennan, c.1996

97   Register of members, 1947–1950

98 Malpass p.133

99 White Paper (Ministry of Housing and Local Government, 1961) published in *Housing in England and Wales* (London: HMSO), cited Malpass p.135

100 Malpass p.136

101 Miss Inglis interview, op. cit.

102 Susan Maclennan *Viewpoint Housing Association, 1947–1997* [unpublished]

103 ibid

Chapter 9 The importance of fund raising

104 Minutes, June 24, 1952

105 Minutes, Eighth Annual General Meeting, March 8, 1955. On this occasion, the Minute also notes that a 'token gift' had been sent to the Churchill Birthday Fund 'in recognition of much legislation beneficial to Housing which had taken place during his term of office'.

106 Minutes, April 12, 1957

107 Minutes, October 31, 1959

108 ibid

109 Minutes, December 19, 1962

110 Miss Ingham presented the 'Week's Good Cause' for BBC Radio on April 30, 1962. The cause is described in the Radio Times as 'Sheltered Living for the Elderly'

111 *Edinburgh Tatler*, July 1967

112 'Running a shop for a housing fund', *Glasgow Herald* November 10, 1967

113 Letter to Etta Whyte from Ian Penman, November 14, 1991

114 Viewpoint Benevolent – report of the year, November 1, 1985

115 It was the sale of the club, on favourable terms, that enabled Viewpoint to purchase and upgrade the shop premises in Bruntsfield.

116 Annual Report 1993–94 p.5

117 Annual Report 1995–96 p.12

118 'Target £1 Million', explanatory document

119 ibid

Chapter 10 Breaking new ground

120 Joan Stephenson, hand-written speech 1997.

121 Malpass p.149

122 ibid p.150

123 ibid p.149

124 Joan Stephenson interview, June 22, 2007

125 Interview, Ian and Elisabeth Penman, October 3, 2007

126 Malpass p.161

127 Tickell p.25

128 Norman Dunhill, quoted in the *The Scotsman*, May 18, 1983 p.14

129 Gillespie Crescent publicity notice, c.1975

130 Charles J Smith *Historic South Edinburgh* (2000: John Donald, Edinburgh) p.73

131 Remains of the original mansion (two door pediments, an 'armorial panel' and a sundial) were discovered during work on the Viewpoint development and donated to the City Museums and Art Galleries. They were placed in the courtyard of Huntly House Museum. (Undated note)

132 Minutes, January 28, 1958

133 Interview, Joan Stephenson, June 22, 2007

134 'House Notes for 6,7 & 8 Inverleith Terrace', written by A. Evelyn Ingham, 1974

135 Interview, Joan Stephenson

136 *The Scotsman* op.cit., May 18, 1983 p.14-15

137 Charles McKean *Edinburgh: an illustrated architectural guide* (1982: Edinburgh, Royal Incorporation of Architects in Scotland, 3rd edition 1983) p.64

138 *Prospect: the Royal Incorporation of Architects in Scotland Quarterly Newspaper* (Issue number 16, Winter 1983), front and back cover spread

139 McKean op.cit. p.109

140 Records of Coats Viyella plc, www.archiveshub.ac.uk/news/02120302.html

141 Lynne Gladstone-Millar *A Century of Caring: the Aged Christian Friend Society of Scotland 1889–1989* (1989: Edinburgh) pp.1 & 12–13

142 Woodthorpe and Old Farm Court were opened in October 1981 by Malcolm Rifkind, MP, then Scottish Minister for Home Affairs and the Environment

143 Viewpoint Report and Accounts for the year to 31st March, 1981: 'Review of the Year'

144 *The Scotsman* op.cit., May 18, 1983 p.14

145 *Fifeshire Journal* November 6, 1862, cited in a letter from Gordon Christie, July 3, 1992

146 Interview, Joan Stephenson

147 Richard Finlay *Modern Scotland 1914–2000* pp.313–4. Moreover, the value of the pension was far lower than many had expected, placing up to three out of ten Scottish pensioners on the poverty line, more than the number of people claiming poor relief on the eve of the Second World War.

148 Viewpoint Report and Accounts for the year to 31st March, 1981: 'Review of the Year'

149 Viewpoint Report and Accounts for the year to 31st March, 1982: 'Review of the Year'

150 Viewpoint Report and Accounts for the year to 31st March, 1983: 'Review of the Year'

151 *The Scotsman* op.cit., May 18, 1983 p.15

Chapter 11 Where there's a will ...

152 Viewpoint Report and Accounts for the year to 31st March, 1986: 'Review of the Year'

153 Viewpoint Housing Association Ltd Annual Report 1993/94 p.1

154 Minutes, Executive Sub-Committee, October 1983

155 Letter from Miss Ingham to Marjory Sinclair, undated 1985

156 Viewpoint Report and Accounts for the year to 31st March, 1986: 'Review of the Year'

157 ibid

158 In addition, Benevolent managed Inverleith Terrace on behalf of Viewpoint Housing.

159 Though this arrangement was evidently an improvement on the 'cordon bleu' meals dished up by Miss P's predecessor.

160 Norman Dunhill, quoted by Susan Maclennan, *Viewpoint Housing Association 1947–1997*

161 The Edinburgh *Evening News*, May 30, 1987

162 Unidentified newspaper cutting, possibly Edinburgh *Evening News*, June 1988

163 Croft-an-Righ summary of arrangements

164 Tickell p.29. Malpass (p.197ff.) outlines the concerns that the new policy raised, including the question of 'whether sufficient private finance would be forthcoming on terms that enabled Housing Associations to carry on building at rents that were affordable to low income households'. Viewpoint's co-ownership arrangement, supported by with loan stock sales, was one way of responding to this issue. However, Malpass also describes a developing situation in which associations now overtook local authorities as the main providers of new rented housing, building relatively large estates occupied mainly by tenants who relied on state benefits for their income. Although Viewpoint was not a big player in this respect, nevertheless, like other associations, it was now subject to increased scrutiny and regulation of the way it managed its affairs.

165 Interview, Henry McIntosh June 7, 2007. Of the original 175 housing units at Kilravock, some have since reverted to traditional social housing. At Croft-an-Righ, the loan stock system didn't have the longevity expected and when the scheme 'transferred engagements' to Viewpoint in 1995, processes were put in place for vacated loan stock apartments to be re-let as fully rented homes.

166 Notes by Norman Dunhill: 'St Raphael's – Nursing Home for the elderly frail and disabled' (undated c.1986)

167 'Building Dossier: St Raphael's, Edinburgh, *Building*, December 8, 1989 pp.49–56

168 Others who recall the gift speak of two sisters. The bequest was administered by lawyers in Glasgow who were not, comments George Home, very forthcoming.

169 Minutes, March 8, 1960

170 Annual Report, 1992–93

Chapter 12 The importance of partnerships

171 In Scotland, the Housing Corporation had been replaced in
April 1989 by Scottish Homes, whose main purpose was to
help provide good housing, in partnership with local
authorities, Housing Associations and other agencies, and
contribute to the regeneration of local communities.
Scottish Homes, with an annual spending capacity of over
£200 million by the turn of the millennium, was funded
through an annual grant from the Government, rental
income, and receipts from the sale of its own houses (see
www.scot-homes.gov.uk/archive). In November 2001,
two years into the existence of a devolved Scottish
administration, most of the functions of Scottish Homes
were transferred to the Executive's new housing and
regeneration agency, Communities Scotland.

172 Annual Report, 1992-3 pp.2–3

173 ibid p.9

174 ibid p.10

175 Minutes, Homes Sub-Committee, July 27, 1993

176 Annual Report, 1995–96 p.3

177 Residents' Newsletter 1997 p.1

178 'New home for Kenneth is more his cup of tea', *Action on
Social Inclusion in Scotland* (Issue 2, September 2000) p.8

179 Annual Report, 1995–96, pp.8–9

180 Dr R Ratcliff, 'Continuity of Care – a strategy for the frail
elderly', internal Viewpoint note dated January 30, 1991. Dr
Ratcliff was a member of the Viewpoint Committee

181 Annual Report, 1996–97, p.8

182 Residents' Newsletter 1997–98 p.1

183 Annual Report 1997–98

184 Annual Report, 2004–05

185 'All farewells should be sudden', *Newspoint*, Summer 2005

186 ibid

Chapter 13 The changing shape of care

187 Communities Scotland register of social landlords at
www.eesystems.communitiesscotland.gov.uk/register

188 *Newspoint* (Autumn 2005) p.2

189 Minutes, St Andrews Community Council (April 2006)
     Appendix C – City Park

190 *Newspoint* (Winter 2007-08) p.3

191 Minutes, St Andrews Community Council (April 2006)
     Appendix C – City Park

192 *Newspoint* (Spring 2006)

193 *Newspoint* (Winter 2005)

194 Karen Croucher et al *Review of Sheltered Housing in Scotland*
     (2008: Scottish Government Social Research at
     www.scotland.gov.uk/socialresearch only)

195 Marjorie Sinclair, Annual Report 1997–98

196 ibid

197 In the Spring 2007 edition of its tenant magazine, *Newspoint*,
     Viewpoint included the diary for one day in the life of a
     Supported Housing Co-ordinator (formerly 'warden'). It
     demonstrates the continuing range and availability of
     Viewpoint's coordinators:

> 9.00 am Start of my day at Cockburn Court. Cleaner is
> on holiday today, so I make sure front and back entrances
> are clean and fresh. Took reading from activity monitor.
>
> 9.30 am Checked laundry rota to see which tenants are
> doing their washing today. Went round to see that they had
> arrived and checked if they needed any assistance.
> Telephoned one tenant to remind her.
>
> Mobile Hairdresser arrives. She has ten regular clients.
>
> Organised Common Room for J D Fashions coming to
> Cockburn Court this morning. They visit us twice per year.
> This is an invaluable service for residents who find difficulty
> getting to the shops for clothes. Laid tables for the Coffee
> Morning.
>
> 10.30 am One resident is coming home from hospital. I
> was there to welcome him back and make sure he got safely
> into his flat and was settled …
>
> Met with Occupational Therapist to discuss the needs
> of one resident and whether they could manage at home
> when discharged from hospital. Lunch 1.00 to 2.00 pm

Checked activity monitors.

2.00 pm Put on my 'TV Engineer's hat' and went to investigate why one tenant's TV was not working. I checked the plug, aerial and handset. HOORAY ... I got the TV to work. The tenant as extremely pleased. 'It's all in a day's work.' My job certainly has lots of variety.

Then I went to visit a resident whose husband is in hospital. I wanted to make sure she was alright and to reassure her.

4.30 pm Nearly time to clock off. I check all windows, doors and laundries. One tenant had forgotten their washing. I folded this and took it to their flat. One last reading of the activity monitor. It is now 5.00pm – time to go home.

198 Interview, Susan Brydon
199 Karen Croucher et al op cit.
200 Interview, Jane Douglas
201 www.eden-alternative.co.uk

Chapter 14 Viewpoint in the future
202 Derek Wanless et al *Securing Good Care for Older People: taking a long-term view* (Wanless Social Care Review) (2006: King's Fund, London) p.xxiii.

'In 2002, around 900,000 older people were considered to have high levels of need, according to the standard assessment of being unable to carry out one or more of the main activities of daily living (ADLs) (being able to wash, dress, feed, toilet, walk and so on). A further 1.4 million older people had low levels of need. Over the 20 years to 2025, the Review projects a rise in the number of older people who do not require care of 44 per cent, a 53 per cent increase in those with some need and a 54 per cent increase in those with a high level of need. Based on expert analysis commissioned for the Review, these increases reflect a future where population health improves due to moderate reductions in obesity and other "lifestyle" conditions, as well as the introduction of effective new treatments or technologies. Overall, the number of people with impairment and dependency will increase significantly over the next 20 years.'

203 Laing & Buisson *Care of Elderly People: Market Survey* 1999, 12th Edition (1999: London) p.1

204 ibid p.7

205 Interview, Margaret Wilkinson

206 Gordon Brown, statement to MPs July 11, 2007

207 BBC news reports: 'Charity backs PM's housing pledge', July 15, 2007 (http://news.bbc.co.uk/1/hi/uk_politics/6899364.stm) and 'Plea to build new council houses', July 12, 2007 (http://news.bbc.co.uk/1/hi/uk/6294274.stm)

208 Archie Stoddart, Director of Shelter Scotland, *The Scotsman* June 22, 2007

209 UK Housing by Tenure statistics in 2007 showed that 10.7 per cent of rentable property was owned by Local Authorities and 8.2 per cent by Housing Associations (Office of National Statistics, cited in BBC report: 'Plea to build new council houses' op cit.

210 Gibb, K 'What future for social housing?' (2007: Inaugural Public Lecture, Faculty of Law, Business and Social Sciences, University of Glasgow) www.gla.ac.uk/departments/urbanstudies/events/pastevents

211 Peter Hetherington, 'The House masters', *The Guardian* December 5, 2007

212 Adam Sampson, Director of Shelter, ibid. Hetherington says that the largest Housing Associations have upwards of 50-60,000 homes on their books. He notes that the Housing Association 'Places for People' describes itself as 'one of the largest property management and development companies in the UK.'

213 Tickell p.2

214 Viewpoint Housing 'Strategic Plan 2007–2010' p.3

215 *Housing Scotland* Issue 32, May 2007 pp.6–7

216 This hybrid approach has not been without its drawbacks. One current member of staff comments that she had not

heard of Viewpoint before joining the organisation, even though she had worked in the care sector for some time. This she attributes largely to the organisation's 'mixed economy'. It doesn't sit neatly under either the social housing or the care home labels and can easily fall 'between two stools'. One of Viewpoint's aims in recent times, therefore, has been to develop a higher public profile.

217 Wanless op. cit. p.xxiii. The report also notes however, that the recent trend in service provision is a move away from relatively 'low-level' services towards more intensive ones. 'This is illustrated by the decline in the number of people who receive home care but an increase in the number of hours of care provided in total.'

218 Interview, Henry McIntosh June 7, 2007